# HAPPYENDINGS

# HAPPYENDINGS

## VOL. II

### 43 CONFESSION'S OF A LOVE GODDESS

written and authored by
# MONI'SOI HUMES

aka #lovegoddess

this book (love x project) gave birth to **moghul life, inc.** love will bring forth the life of your seed in due season you shall bring forth life

# #lovewins

# COPYRIGHT PAGE

© 2016 by Moni'soi Humes

All rights reserved according to UCC 1-308. No part of this publication may be reproduced, distributed, or transmitted in any form or by any means, including photocopying, recording, or other electronic or mechanical methods, without the prior written permission of the publisher, except in the case of brief quotations embodied in critical reviews and certain other noncommercial uses permitted by copyright law. For permission requests, write to the publisher, addressed "Attention: Permissions Coordinator," at the email address below under Orders.
Moghul Life, Inc {Publishing}

Ordering Information:
Quantity sales. Special discounts are available on quantity purchases by corporations, associations, public relation & advertising agencies, and others. For details, contact the publisher at the address above.

Orders by US trade bookstores and wholesalers. Please contact Heaven on Earth, Inc., Publishing Department: mhumes@live.com rbragency@gmail.com or visit Author's website www.monisoihumes.co Booking the Author for speaking engagements, events, and book signings. Email rbragency@gmail.com
Printed in the United States of America
Publisher's Cataloging-in-Publication data
Moni'soi Humes

**Happy Endings/Subtitle 43 Confession's of a Love Goddess/VOL II/Moni'soi Humes;**

ISBN 13: 978-0692629987 (Moghul Life, Inc)
ISBN-10: 069262998X

1. The main category of the book —Self Help/Relationships —Love 2.

Printed in the United States of America

When you give life a chance, love will show you that you are more than worthy of what it has to offer you even past your own insecurities. Trust in love, because love trusts in you.

about 43 confessions of a love goddess
introduction 1(43)
confession #1
confession #2
confession #3
confession #4
confession #5
confession #6
confession #7
confession #8
confession #9
confession #10
confession #11
confession #12
confession #13
confession #14
confession #15
confession #16
confession #17
confession #18
confession #19
confession #20
confession #21
confession #22
confession #23
confession #24
confession #25

confession #26

confession #27

confession #28

confession #29

confession #30

confession #31

confession #32

confession #33

confession #34

confession #35

confession #36

confession #37

confession #38

confession #39

confession #40

confession #41

confession #42

confession #43

afterword

authors bio

*you are a god*
*you are a goddess*

*enter into my confessions*

# About 43 Confessions of a Love Goddess

43 Confessions of a Love Goddess was formed and created from a mere passion and desire to release love unto the people that read it {You}. A god and goddess is a lower version of God, it is your ability to be aware of the higher consciousness of self. This awareness is what will allow you to flow with the rhythm and the vibrations of the love that is within you. It will increase your ability to connect with yourself, your partner, and the universe.

It is understood that life will still continue to happen due to the fact that it is just life. You are blessed to have good days and you are blessed to have bad days, both in which make your life completely interesting. As challenging as life can be it can serve you days that make you want to throw in the towel, however the little nudge that you can feel tugging on you from within is love letting you know that you have something to fight for. When the time comes for you to embrace that moment it will happen naturally and there is nothing that you can do about love loving the hell out of you.

We all have something that we may or may not want to confess, well love is my confession. Love has been at the forefront of my desire for as long as I can remember. This book is to be read with joy, hope, and a peace that the **power of the love** that is in you will in fact come out. I ask that the love that is in you is released in the atmosphere. Every page that you turn, every confession that you read, and that all pain that you have experienced in your past will be broken off of your life. Prepare yourself to reach the ultimate level of happiness.

# 1(43)

## Introduction to 43 Confessions of a Love Goddess

The goal of this book is to share with you my story as a woman. It was written as a way to help men to understand us more and a way to help women to trust in love more. I have seen many things in my life as woman. I wrote this book based off of my own experiences, situations that I have observed from watching others, and from some of the individuals that taught moi how to love truly.

The truth is that ladies I know that you are hurting like hell and it does not help that every woman that you have ever trusted to teach you how to be the ideal woman of virtue for your man has completely failed you. But the truth is that is ok and everything is going to be all right. I as well had to learn it all the hard way. I had to learn from trial and error. If I could do it all again some of that shit I really wouldn't. I would have made better decisions for my own life. Of course we have all heard of the saying, "*Live with no regrets.*" I would be completely lying if I didn't have any. I do believe that life is supposed to be lived without regrets, but we don't actually know that we are going to regret the decision that we are making while we are making it. If we did life would be a whole lot easier. There is a reason that I went through the things that I went through. It was to become the woman that would share with you how awesome you can be to yourself as a female and how awesome you can be for your man.

    We dump so much off on men, mainly all of our thoughts, all of our feelings, and spiritually most men are not equipped to handle the emotions that we as woman dish out. Right men? Meanwhile we are doing the dishing and he is in mental overload, zoned out in a different space that has nothing to do with you. And you put him there.

Men deal with so much on a daily basis and it must be known that it is way too much for him to come home to a place that lacks peace and to have to deal with the only woman that wants to add more to his back. When he comes home you should have not only prepared a place for him but you should have open arms to him. You should be in your purest state of mind ready and willing to please your guy, because that is the only thing that he needs from you when he has had a long day.

Yes, I understand that you had a long day too, but pray, and find a friend that truly cares about your well being enough to listen to you. Have some type of release for yourself that way when you see him you are not giving him all that junk. So many woman have great men and they treat them like their past, what they have been through, and what other no good men have done to them. Men deserve your love, your loyalty, and most importantly your respect.

What happened was that some overly spiritual woman told you to save yourself for that one perfect guy, not give him sex, and not enjoy any type of fun with him. This is what I call old school religion and most often it never works for the current situation that you are in. Why? Because you and your guy are already having sex, in fact you are having lots of it, every chance the two of you get. Sex is what the two of you desire to do. The only problem on a religious end is that you are mentally and spiritually warring in your mind if you are pleasing unto God. It puts a thought in your mind that God is Un-enjoyable, Un-pleasing, and that the spirit knows nothing about love making at all. This is so not the truth. Why would 'goddess beings' lack all sexual desire to please their partner? Most of what we have learned does not makes any sense, not to our lives, and definitely not to the life of your partner. The truth is individuals in whom have been giving you advice for years have only been destroying relationships. I will not number the amount of older, religious women that I took advice from that meant moi no good. Of course it was not intentional, but some of them live in a time warp that has noting to do with living in this generation.

Men you on the other hand deal with things differently. The thing is that you feel like you have a hard time trying to figure us out, well dido! We feel the same way. We have absolutely no idea as to what you are thinking. There are many days where women are like WTF is he thinking? You guys are quiet when it comes to how you feel. Ladies want to be comforted by the comforting words of her guy. She wants you to reassure her when she is unsure about something. Your words give her power, faith, and more confidence in the relationships. Your words will keep her in a place of confidence. And throw out the idea that women are jealous, they are not. Jealousy is something that you feel when someone has something that you do not have and you desire to have it. Women are territorial creatures, their nature is similar to that of an animal. She protects what is hers even when you don't accept that she is doing so.

Both of you are challenged at this point to take a deep breathe and open yourself to reading about love and how the two of you both can reach a happy ending in your relationship. Give in to the love.

# confession 1

## WHEN A WOMAN IS FED UP IT IS OVER WITH

*"We spend our entire life seeking love that it is hidden deep inside of us all. Some show it! And some release the inner beast."*

If you asked moi years ago what my first thought of men was I would have said, *"I can't stand men and that most of them are idiots."* I am pretty sure that both the male and female has felt this at some point towards their counterpart. Men just verbalize the word Bitch instead of idiot. We are saying the same shit. But you know what they say about when a women's fed up. R. Kelley sang it best. #WhenAWomensFedUp there is nothing you can do about it. In my case this time I began writing about my 43 Confessions of love, relationships, and all of the non-sense we encounter on the way.

When you get sick and tired of being sick and tired you will do something about it. I know that life is about growing as a woman, but somehow I could not

# WHEN A WOMANS FED UP THERE IS NOTHING YOU CAN DO ABOUT IT
-R. Kelley

get the understanding of this relationship thing under wraps. I mean if God created relationships, *"Why could I not figure them out?"* I am just saying, either love is my gift or my curse. Either way I was beginning to not like either one.

    I can't assure that you will receive the answers that you are looking for by reading this book. Well, wait, hold on!

## LOVE DISCLAIMER

What you are about to read is some real life experiences, however do not be alarmed that I went through it. In life there are no guaranteed

**answers. Just be prepared to keep going no matter what you are faced with.**

Anyway I hope that you are ready, because I really had to get personal with how I was feeling within myself. If you know moi then you will know that normally my personal life is not up to be shared with anyone. I was learning through trial and error that some things just ticked moi off about relationships and men. I did not understand why a man would give you straight hell and still walk around like he is the man. And for the life of moi I could not get why some men felt superior by ordering women around just off of the strength of being a man. What amazes moi is the fact that there are so many rich men bullies who think the answer to everything is money. Until they meet a woman who says, "*No*." Ladies you must stand your ground with men or they will treat you like they hired you to be a face that shows up when they want to show off.

Men we don't mind being beautiful on your side, but we are not toys. We do have brains and there is nothing that we would not do for you when you show us the love that we desire. We will give you all the respect that you need and desire. All you have to do is lead the way.

I knew in my heart of hearts that a real man lives by the truth, and with love. He will not have an excuse to mistreat you. Some men verbally abuse women and blame it on the truth and you cannot tell them anything, because they look at you as one who is clueless. Deep down inside he operates more in religion that you think. His desire is for you to obey. An individual can obey God through their obedience of what is purposed for their life, however religion is just another form of slavery and a trap that was put in place to get the people to rebel. Rebellion is another reason for people to do what they want as they hide behind the name God to get you to obey them instead of the real truth.

Ladies are not exempt from anything I am saying I am just speaking on the fact that some times your woman is right fellas and you just don't want to listen to her, because you are looking through the eyes of religion instead of the eyes of love. You know how that goes, so the two of you are spending time fighting for the attention of the other person. Yet both of you are playing the "dumb game." He says, *"You know how many would love to be with a King?"*

You respond with the same non sense, *"You are lucky that I am even with you, there are so many men who would love to be in a relationship with moi and walk in being King."* As the two of you play the game back and forth, not realizing that the two of you are lacking the wisdom of love. These words are destroying your bond, your union, and your love.

The funny part of it is that the two of you probably don't even love one another, but wont confess it because the spirit of pride is at work instead of humility.

When you are in love, you will feel vulnerable. Love is a very special place that allows the two of you to be intimate. God has given us this love to be able to share this intimacy with our partner.

I made a decision when it came to love, one that many of us made once we have enough. I decided that God could not want for moi to be in a relationship. He must have meant for moi to write about my relationship with him-Right?

All I knew was at some point I wanted the story to end-period. Point blank! No, if, and's, nor buts about it. I still had a lot of learning to do. Now I wonder often if I was set up by God to be in situations that would one day inspire moi to do what I am doing now. Writing. My life had been designed by God to help others.

**"Greater hath no man than this, that a man lay down his life for his friend." John 15:13**

This meant that the love that you have within yourself is not just for you. Again, *"No greater love than to lay your life down for a friend."*

Now when you are angry the last thought you are thinking is laying down your life for the idiot that you are standing in front of or Bitch. Whatever moment you are in. Excuse moi, but when you are upset you say things. You say mean things. It is easy when you are in your feelings to just be emotional and as mean as you possibly can. All human beings deep down inside desire to feel some type of love. We were created for this purpose.

Psychologist have concluded that the need to feel loved is a primary human emotional need. According to the 5 Love Languages the heart will experience the following for the sake of love:

1. Climb Mountains
2. Cross seas
3. Travels across deserts
4. Endure untold hardships
5. Mountains become inclinable
6. Seas un-crossable
7. Deserts un-bearable
8. Hardships our lot in life

It is amazing what one human being would do just for the sake of love. It is amazing how far they would go and how hard they are willing to make things work just for the sake and in the name of love. No one can give you the ability to love someone like this, when you do love someone like this just be prepared for the climbing of mountains, the crossing of seas, the travels across desserts, and the endurance of good times and bad times. Just keep going. Keep loving your partner by listening and being sensitive to their suggestions, needs, and desires. When I did not know how to love I received great suggestions on how to embrace the gift of love and I only rejected it just to find out that maybe if I embraced the lesson sooner the road would not have been so hard. A hard head will get you no where fast. Stop that shit immediately!

# confession 2
## LOOK IN THE MIRROR, YOU ATTRACTED THEIR ASS

Psychology has a lot to do with our relationships, our behavior, our attitude, and our perception of life. Our past also plays a part in how we effectively communicate with our partner. Most partners have no idea why they are fighting, yet both are of equal importance, and neither of them are listening to one another.

This is why we make-up, break up, and start over. As for moi I just did not know how to exercise patience. I guess in a way I did, since I dealt with so much non-sense already. It is a wonder why I was able to still have a heart to love, however I do. Love has kept my heart open. Open to life, love, and the universe.

**Love is real.**

Question is,
*"What exactly do you love about yourself?"*
You cannot love someone else until you fall in love with who you are.

## RULES WERE MEANT TO BE BROKEN

You grow up being taught that you would have this perfect life. You thought that when you got older you would have a partner that would love you for an eternity, kids, a big, beautiful house, and two luxury vehicles in your two car garage, and a sports car for fun on the weekends. The great thing is that you are still alive to make that happen.

The problem is that it does not quite work like that. I wish! Love is something that must be worked at. Everything that I wanted, I had. But those were only material things: When I lost those things I had to learn what real love meant. My experience in life with men was that the men who have the most, sometimes are the ones who will treat you the worst. The ones with less well are even worse. It is important to be in a relationship with a partner who is balanced from within. Haha then of course I have to take my advice I must have been somewhat cold myself. I really had some growing to do. But also know that sometimes you can get in a relationship with someone that was never meant to be part of your life. Kick their ass out! Now!

It is so easy for a man or a woman to be scorned from their past that they often end up scorning the one that they are with. They make their current partner pay for another person's mistakes and it is so unfair.

Life began teaching moi that all these rules, systematic way of doing things need to be broken off of our lives, and off the lives of those trusting that love is theirs. There are generational curses, traditional curses, racial curses, cultural curses, and religious curses.

Romeo and Juliet is a Shakespeare love story that we are all familiar with. Their love was filled with so much passion, suffering, and drama. It became the love story of all time because of how it ended.

*"The subtle outrageousness of Shakespeare's drama is that everything is against the lover' their families & the state, the indifference of nature, the vagaries of time, and the regressive movement of the cosmological contraries of love and strife." –*
**William Shakespeare**

Passion is so strong when mixed with love. It is an emotion that is so strong that it is barely controllable. It is intense. It is great to have passion for your partner, the problem is that passionate individuals over do their love for you. Their passion is so strong that they just have to release it some type of way. If it is not pure love then the passion will be negative and not positive.

Passion is released through:

1. Affection
2. Attention
3. Intercourse
4. Gifts
5. Kindness
6. Communication

7. Finances
8. Engaging words, poetry
9. Candle lite dinners
10. Nice trips
11. Love letters & notes
12. Walks in the park
13. Anger (negative)
14. Hatred (negative)
15. Violence (negative)
16. A bad temper (negative)
17. Do as I say attitude (negative)
16. Harm and danger (negative)

What is so weird is that passion possesses the characteristics of love, hate, and this will often lead to separation. Romeo and Juliet had an equal amount of passion for one another. This is a very rare relationship, typically it is the other way around usually one partner has more passion than the other. Ok they took their passion to the extreme. They took one another out. I don't know about you, but hey to each is own.

In order to make a relationship work we must find a balance. A harmonious place where the two of you can rest in. When a scale is off balance it goes up and down, so will you and your partner when you don't work on bringing a balance into your relationship, and your life.

**HOW DO YOU CREATE BALANCE INTO YOUR LIFE & YOUR RELATIONSHIP?**

1. Prayer

2. Find a common ground, focus on that area

3. Create a goal that you can achieve together as partners. {This will form a unique bond and bring the two of you fulfillment.}

4. Meditate. We often meditate alone, however it should become a spiritual practice to do so together at least

once out of the week as this creates a harmony that syncs the two of you with a stronger bond.

5. Study together. This will remove confusion when the two of you are on the same page. Sometimes you will meet a partner that has a natural awareness. Don't force any of this on them, grow yourself first. They will want to know what you are doing.

6. Eat together. This helps bond the two of you together, if you have a family everyone should do this together. *"When you're belly is being satisfied, communication is peaceful."*

7. Work on a project together

8. Have a date night at least once out of the week

9. Learn their language

{According, to the "5 Love Languages" we all love differently}[1]

a. Love Language #1 Words of Affirmation
b. Love Language #2 Quality Time
c. Love Language #3 Receiving Gifts
d. Love Language #4 Acts of Service
e. Love Language #5 Physical Touch

I must make this confession I want it all, however if I had to choose two I would say that Word of Affirmations and Quality Time mean the most to moi. Wink! Wink! I love gifts too though.

Words can either make you or break you. I am a words lover, love moi through words of affirmations and show moi acts of service while you do. I love being served. I am a spoiled brat sometimes. I had to take my time with choosing this one, I was fighting

---

[1] The Five Love Languages, The Secret to Love that Lasts by Dr. Gary Chapman

between Love Language # 3 & Love Language #4, however I chose the two that were most like my love.

## LOVE LAW

*"You must love your partner in the way that they desire to be loved, not the way that you desire to be loved. Love is about us, not about I."*

In order to do this you must learn to listen to them as they teach you how to love them. The worst thing you can tell your partner is I am just going to be moi regardless of how you feel, because that sounds to them like "I, I, and more I." You have to be sensitive enough to not be someone else, but to be considerate enough that you have a person in your life that loves completely different from you do. If they are considerate enough to give you the love that you need then do the same. Don't let them be in a one sided relationship alone. Show them that you appreciate them just as much as they appreciate you. If one partner is going out of his or her way to be in a relationship with you this is dangerous. It works when a relationship is new however that person will eventually feel like someone would be willing to go the extra mile like they are. Don't lose the greatest person of your life by not paying attention to their needs. This is selfish of you. There are many people who lose wonderful individuals all because their partner took them for granted. Some of the greatest individuals are appreciated long after they are gone.

In conclusion sometimes we may feel clueless as to who our partner is, but if we find balance we can learn to love them for who they are and not for the way you desire to be loved. Start putting yourself in your partner shoes. To truly love your partner is to take your eyes off of yourself and embrace the way that they love. Remember you did not find out who you were in one day then why would you expect them after months, a year, or even years to know everything about you. It takes time to know yourself and it takes time for your partner to get to know you. Embrace the attraction. Embrace the love.

Culture has played a major role in your love life.

# confession 3
## THIS IS THE PART WHERE I SAY FUCK LOVE

## YOU CAN'T HELP WHO YOU LOVE CAN YOU?

We have been taught year after year that we are connected to one human being for the rest of our life, well that can be boring especially since it may not be true. It seems so easy to follow taught rituals without ever learning what personally works for you. There are several factors that you can look at that can help you "*help*" who you love. All these traditions do is get us into a world of trouble that we don't know how to get ourselves out of.

We all know:
God will send a man.

God will show you the type of woman that you desire. There is a huge difference between a wife and a woman. There is also a difference between a man and a husband. You will be able to distinguish the difference through their characteristics. There is also a huge difference between a King and a man, a Queen and a woman, and god and a goddess.

Therefore to add injury to insult, none of us have any influence in the decision of who they are with when it comes to traditions. We live in a world of culture and we are all supposedly doing the same thing, following the same principles that are spoken unto us all in different languages with a different voice and a different culture.

The Japanese culture believes that pre-arranged marriages are less likely to end up in divorce, whereas those in love will be more likely to divorce. The Indian culture also lives in similar culture where a man's wife is chosen for him. I watched a someone close to moi who is Indian fly to India to marry a woman that he barely knew because of traditions. Although he grew up in America, his family still wanted him to live according to their families traditions even at the cost of their son being with a woman that he did not love. It is amazing how many people have to live this life with no regards to what is in their heart. It is not just in the Indian culture, because many Americans and other cultures do the same thing by not approving of someone that their son or daughter may love based on their culture, race, background, and their difference. It is sad that we go through this but this is what contributes to a lack of love in today's society and no one wants to admit that they need to live their own life, not the life of history, not their parent's life, not their past life, but their own life. You deserve to be happy now. Don't give away your happiness to please someone else. It is not worth the hassle.

    Marriages in Japan that are performed by religious or fraternal bodies are meaningful for most people, but are considered legal marriages.

    Marriages this way are easier to deal with, because the emotions are completely absent from the marriage. Individuals who marry for love have more issues to work past and through according to their cultural difference. When you are in love, passion will rise up to make you feel a certain way. The way that Japanese go about marriage there is no need for emotions, arguments, disagreements because it is organized just as a business deal. They are pre-chosen for one another. They entire a contract of obligation verses one of love. This is why my perception of marriage has changed. The purpose of contracts is to make sure that the other person holds up their end of the deal. When you are in love and you are spiritually connected there should be no need for a contract. You are married the day that the two of you chose to have sex. At that moment the two of you became one.

    Culture is just a system of beliefs that we have usually from our family. Here is the thing with those who don't have that particular type of culture is the fact that sometimes we go through life, relationships, and we build with a partner that we don't even know if God has pre-chosen that person for us. It takes two making a decision from within to see if the person that they are about to connect to has qualities and or characteristics to live a life of love together. Sometimes the more you learn about a person, the more you find out that you cannot stand them at all.

And sometimes the more you learn about them, the more that you love them altogether.

It is extremely important before you get serious that you know the family of your partner. This will reveal their curses and their blessings before you get a chance to see it manifest in your partner. It will manifest. Trust moi when I say this. We have our parents DNA, somewhere along the road we repeat our parents mistakes or we learn from our parents mistakes. But when you are serious about someone it is definitely important to know at least some of their family before you dive all in.

In my younger days: One of my ex a year and a half after we started dating took moi to meet his parents. No biggie. Right? A man waits before he introduces you to his parents until he is serious about you? At least this is what I thought. No worries right and I did not even give it a second thought.

His parents fought, cursed, yelled, and damn near made it feel like they wanted to kill one another. This was an extremely high level of passion that was filled with negativity, and un-resolved issues. This was a sign of abuse, one that I ignored, besides my man was in the church, a deacon, and a choir singer, and a provider, there was no point of ending a great thing. He was all that I needed and wanted, at least I thought. I cared for him very deeply. He took great care of moi. He showed moi a different life. He showed moi what I could do on my own. He should moi that I was capable of anything that I could possibly put my mind too. He just had another side to who he was.

One day I saw his temper and told him that I could not allow myself to be brought down by any one, especially not a man. I let him go, but my heart was caught up, and eventually he got back into my heart. I loved him very dearly, but there were still signs and they were screaming, *"Hello, I know you see me."* However my dumb ass went all in, I wanted him to be mine forever. I loved him when I laid down at night and when I woke up. He was the provider, protector, business man, role man, & the person that I desired to be in my life so I overlooked the bad. Whatever temper he had as long as he didn't touch moi I could deal with it. Then one day he put his hands on moi. He choked moi. The babysitter was at the house that summer, she heard us in the bedroom, and called the police. The police told moi that they thought I should consider moving they said they had a little sister and would tell her the same, *"This guy won't change. He will probably do it again."*

    This was not the first time that I saw him angry. He did get angry before, but he would take it out on a door or something else. I thought forever meant forever with him. I thought that you can't help who you love. I didn't want to help it. My life was better than most people that I knew my age. I wanted it to work. I just did not know the signs.

What are signs of a curse? Signs are always alerting you, just pay attention, and get out when you see them. When you go all in, it makes it hard later.

    ***Sign #1 Mental & Physical Abuse*** {I should have

    Titled this book, *"Relationships from hell, depart to Heaven"* LMAO!

Hey, I have seen better days, met better people, but what I could not figure out was why I was so in love with this man. I had to ask myself, "Why?" The abuse got worse, and I eventually allowed the situation to cause me to hit rock bottom. The problem was the fact that I was such a dependent woman, a stay at home mother. Having to face life was hard, a broken heart, no where to go, and to explain to my kids that everything would be ok when I did not even know if that was true. I was angry, mad at God. I knew God could have shielded us from the pain, but I didn't understand why God allowed it to get so bad.

Other signs of curses that I saw with my own two eyes:

### Sign #2 Alcoholism curse

Whenever you attend a family gathering of a potential partner or someone in whom you are dating and the family members think that there is a reason every time to pull out a 12 pack of beer and to take a ride to the liquor store. This is weekly. No breaks! There is nothing wrong with drinking, but we all know an alcoholic that will blow the fun for everyone with another shot. I mean like damn they can't just drink and enjoy being social, they want to curse people out, and get into trouble for whatever reason that is only apparent to them alone.

### *Sign #3 Mommy dearest is the Breadwinner!*

Mom is the bread winner of the home and there is certainly nothing wrong with this picture, but if all pressure falls back on her there is a problem. Yes, we live in an independent society, however in my book a man should have the God given ability to take care of his Queen, his home, and kids if he has any. God created men to be providers. The man should not depend on his woman to live. Woman should not depend on man to live, they should build together in unison.

### *Sign #4 Irresponsible curse*

You don't want to rule your partner out completely, there is still a chance for him or her to get things right.

Men who live at home with parents: If your partner lives at home with Mom and Dad, he is still walking in the role of being son, and he is probably hiding a few skeletons in his closet that he does not see. Pay attention! No shade! Only truth! How can you take care of a woman when you are still living in a faulted system? Now I am not against anyone being at home, things happen. However if you have no intentions of being out of this situation and you are completely comfortable with this situation never changing that is a problem. Same thing goes for her, she has to get her life together before she even tries to worry about a man. But when it is meant to be the two of you will get a plan together, work it together, and build it together.

If you are in a relationship with this man, know that he is pulling you back as God prepares you for your launch.

I have spent some years being childish this I know, but there comes a point, and a season when you become a woman or a man of purpose. You cannot run to your parents every time your partner makes you mad. If your man or woman is like this, 9 x out 10 he or she will not make a good lifetime partner. Build with someone who has cut the umbilical cord. Learn to work out your problems between the two of you without outsiders dragging you.

**Sign #5 She is a fucking complainer.**

She spends her time telling her problems to as many women that will listen to her. She is always talking about what he is doing. She does not exist to herself. If she did then she would know that she has just as many issue in her own damn life that she needs to check. She lacks trust in who she is.

She is addicted to getting help, but she does not really want it. These type of women get addicted to living disarrayed lifestyles. Even when she acknowledges that wisdom of what is being said she returns back to a state of confusion. She will be ok for weeks, but give her some time and she will return back to an even worse state.

**Curse #6 Bad Bitch**

Ok! Whatever! I don't get it. You hate it when a man refers to you as a bitch, but that is your nickname. In order to get respect you must first establish a connection between having respect and loving yourself. This type of female when she sees her homegirl, *"Whats up Bitch?"* Now as a female I know that this is completely harmless. The problem exists in the power of our language, because if you continue to refer to yourself as such then you are also bound to attracting the same type of vibration into your life. When he calls you a Bitch and you have a problem the first thing your guy will say is that he heard you referring to yourself as a Bitch.

The power of who we are is in our tongue first. Check the words that you are releasing into the atmosphere. If you want love and respect there are some things that you are going to have to change from your language and your actions. Actions are preceded by the words, *"I am a Bad Bitch."* No worries though, because there is someone for everyone. *"I love bad bitches, that is my fucking problem, and yeah I like to fuck that is my fucking problem."* **2 Chainz**

There are all just different attitudes and personalities of individuals who live with *"Fuck Love,"* on their mind so it becomes their lifestyle. People have so many different characteristics and personality traits. Below are characteristics that I personally don't like.

Characteristics that I personally think will never survive the likes of a relationship with moi long. I personally cannot stand these traits:

> **"I love bad bitches, that is my fucking problem, and yeah I like to fuck that is my fucking problem."**
> -2Chainz

• **Arrogance** – you cannot tell this personality type nothing, they know everything.

• **Ego** – they just need to be right all the time for the sake of being right. Stupidity!

- **Pride** – they know that they are wrong, however will insist on saying, *"I am not wrong and I don't care who does not like it."* Their plot in life is about them. You will not win with them so stop trying. It was not meant to happen.

Mean while, as they walk out the room, you begin to have your thoughts, *"I cannot stand this motherfucker."* Excuse my language. Forgive moi God, but you know that this person is an absolute unbearable person to deal with, not to mention there is no room for a help meet in this man's life. He already knows everything, and any help he needs, he gets on his own. He will rule you to be of no importance to his life every time.

The question is, *"Can you help who loves you?"* No! You can't help who loves you or who you love, but you can help who you decide to spend your life with. As human beings it is so natural for us to care for those who need us, however it is un-natural for us to go into a relationship with that same exact thought. When you are in a committed relationship there should be an understanding of fulfilling one another's need together.

You must ask yourself, *"What do you desire and whom do you desire?"* We do the same thing when we make professional decisions by weighing our options, looking at the pro's and the cons, yet when it comes to relationships we just jump in head first, and think later. In return our personal life suffers. I experienced this the hard way. Be friends with a person as long as you can first before you ever even go on a date with them. Friendships are life long when they are real. This is a great way to get to know a person before you decide to spend your life with them. I do believe that there are rare occasions of experiencing love at first sight, however it is very rare that this will happen. I know, I use to live there. Dreamland, Hello!

## You will never experience the fullness of love until you take fear out of the equation.

You know what you want, stop living in fear, and get it. Stop thinking about what your family will say, what you friends will say, and what your co-workers will say. You will never experience the fullness of love until you take fear out of the equation.

There is this person in your life who you have been seeing for a long time, but you know that if you stay with them this individual will continue to make you feel like you have been the only cause for their problems. Until a person knows for themselves that something needs to change, they will not change it. For the life of the situation stop believing that you have the power to change any individual that has no desire to create change within themselves.

Each partner needs to be consciously aware of the other partner. If not both partners will begin to feel alone and empty within the relationship. This is not good, this means that your relationship could be taking a turn for the worse. When individuals say that they are feeling alone in a relationships, somewhere along the line being their for one another was taken off of the table.

It is a bad feeling to feel your partner does not have any care or concern for how you feel. It is an awful feeling to have someone in your life, yet to feel they are not even there. What is even worse is knowing that the person that you are with has not even picked up on how bad you are feeling on the inside, this is why you can very much help who you love.

Only give that special place in you that should belong only to your soulmate to that special someone. That person should make you feel like you have entrusted your heart with a partner that is equally responsible for any damage that can be created between the two of you. The two of you are the only ones who can repair what the two of you damaged. Love is formed through an equal bond.

When someone you care about has an, *"I don't care attitude toward you and your relationship that is exactly what it means."*

They care less about what you are feeling. They understand that you are hurting, but they don't want to get rid of their pride to find out why.

This relationship is doomed unless the other partner comes to realize that they are hurting the two of you. In order for this to happen their soul has to be intertwined with God. *"Don't waste your life with a person that does not mind wasting your time."* A man and a woman should have a plan for their time.

## LOVE LAW

*" Know that whatever is done by one is done equally to your love."*

I want this book to heal homes, to mend broken hearts, and to help couples share their most intimate moments and thoughts with their partner. *"No one wants to be alone unless they are seeking true happiness."*

There is a true mis-conception that when individuals decide to be alone that they are miserable. This is only a myth! They just desire to seek their own happiness. They learn to have a relationship with self or with God. If they decide to share that intimate space with another it will be someone that shares the same intimate relationship with God that they do.

This book is truly unfiltered for the purpose of helping those who are walking in the same shoes that I walked in.

I must continue to say what the people in this world wonder. We have been lied to for centuries. We have been told that there is no Mr. or Mrs. Right for you. That was a lie! Mr. & Mrs. Right exist in a space that is only known to God, to them, and to both individuals that that love exists in. Come on, keep reading! I have some crazy shit to tell you.

# confession 4
## DAMN DID THIS DUDE JUST BREAK IN MY HOUSE

"The funny thing is that the shit really happened. Some people do real dumb shit all the time. Period!"

Damn this dude is on the ground. I wonder is his ass dead? If he is I am about to pull off and that is exactly what I did. I cannot believe that I caught him stealing my flat screen out of my house. He was carrying it out of the front door. As he was about to put the TV on the back of his truck, I simply put my car in reverse then in drive, and slightly bumped his thieving ass, and he landed on the hood of my car. Once I realized that he was not moving I pulled off, he fell to the ground, and I called my mom in panic.

"*Mom he is dead,*" I said.

*"What calm down! Who is dead? What are you talking about?*

"I am talking about-well I won't mention his name here, but he broke into my house, he was stealing my TV, and I backed the car up in reverse, and I think that I hit him. I think that he is dead!"

I really did not think that he was dead but I was in panic mode. I could not for the life of moi figure out why someone that I cared for would break into my house and make my ass feel uncomfortable at any point. I had some shit to learn in my life and I was about to learn it real quick, this dude was not wasting anytime with the bull shit.

My mother replied again, *"Calm down, go back to your house, and call 911. Do it now!"*

"OK," I said. Then I hung the phone up, called my friend, a told him what happened, and he said, *"Go back to the house. He broke in. You won't be in trouble. You were protecting yourself. It is illegal to break in someones' house. You just need to calm down. It will be all right."* Maybe it was the tone in his voiced that convinced moi that everything would work out just fine.

I went back to the house but by that time I had arrived he was in the neighbors yard laying on the ground. My first thought was, *"How did he get his ass over there?"* The police were pulling up when I got there, so were the ambulance. The police began to question moi and I told them what happened.

Their response was, *"Your fine, this guy has a record, and some bad habits, and we are not particularly fond of him. He has a warrant, so once he gets checked out at the hospital, we will take him to jail."* OK, this was a rude awakening. How did I miss all of this? On top of that this is one of those instances where I thought love at first sight existed. Damn this dude's game was real strong.

So after they got all my information, he was put inside of the ambulance, and the police came back to make sure that I was all right.

Then I thought about something, about prior situation. Previously I had a ticket, my best friend had recently passed away, and my license were suspended. I had completely forgot about it, because I was morning the death of my friend. The judge had given me community service, and if you know moi when I was younger that was not going to happen.

When I thought about it, I got back in my car, pulled off just to see an officer put on his sirens. I pulled over, the officer gets out of the car, and says, *"Miss, I know that you have been having a hard day, but there is also a warrant for your arrest, but if you pay $1500 you will be released right away."*

Now I am in the back of the police car. I call my mom to tell her that I was going to jail and she says, *"He was dead?"*

*"No, I had a warrant also. The bond is $1500, but I will just go sit until I see the judge."* Besides I had some shit on my mind. Shit my house had just got broken in to, I did not feel safe there, and I really did not want to be around my family. Shit was heavy. I really did not want anyone to see moi like that.

That is what I did. I needed time to think and I really wanted to be away from the world. Hey everyone has a past and everyone has a present. This was a Saturday afternoon, and I sat there until Tuesday. My fine was paid on that day when I left, I left with a clear mind, and vowed to never let this man return into my life. What could be worse than the person that you are in love with stealing from you? Well, it gets worse I found out later that he was on Cocaine. I had no knowledge of this. He went to work Monday – Saturday at 5 am, this made no sense. I was clueless of the signs.

The problem was that later on he was not over me. He was charged with stalking; he broke in my house again, stole my car keys to my Volvo, stole my cash, and broke my flat screen in the living room, and my computer as well. At this point I literally had no feelings for this man whatsoever. My feelings disappeared. Some individuals will just do so much shit that you will feel absolutely nothing for them any longer. This was that situation.

What got moi in the first place, was the fact that he was sweet as ever when I first met him. He took moi dancing, cooked for moi, and he handled his business. All of this changed, he got back on drugs which was something that I never knew of in the first place. Why, because I believed that love at first sight existed.

I began to wonder, *"Was this what love was all about?"* If so it was not for moi, I told myself that I would never love anyone ever again. Well, those were my emotions. Besides how could I give up on such a beautiful treasure from God?

My problem at this point was the fact that instead of getting better I went for worse, and this is how the story of the 43 Confessions of a Love Goddess was created. This is when I realized why I was attracting men with bad habits. I really just wanted to spend my life with a man who loves God, who values moi, and someone that I could talk to, and even lean on when times were hard.

Every woman and man no matter what their background is wants a ride or die for life that is just the way that it is. No one wants someone who gives up when the going gets tough. No one wants someone who walks away every time shit don't go their way. Life is about holding on for as long as you can until you get the results that you desire.

# confession 5

## MEN + WOMEN KEEP RESUMES ON FILE

"Girl don't answer the phone. People just call to see if their resume is still on file. If you answer a call from your ex, he knows he is still on file."

In loving memory of Shannon Hendricks, I speak of her a lot because she will always mean a lot to moi.

Shannon was my best friend. She passed away many years ago. She was a great friend who listened to moi, made moi laugh, laughed with moi, and who cared dearly for moi. We talked on the phone whenever we were not together. On this one particular day she said to moi, *"Girl you have to be like moi when it comes to relationships."*

"How is that?"

*"Girl you know when your ex calls you and you have not spoken to one another in a while,"* she answered.

*"Yes,"*

*"Girl they are not calling to check on you, they are calling to see if they still have their resume on file. When they stop calling you it is because either they moved on with their life or you stop answering their calls. Men will love you one day and be with someone else the next. Remember that."*

This shit was the funniest thing that I ever heard, but Shannon was a Pisces she was straight up about the shit she said and the shit that she knew. If you know moi, you know that Pisces are the fish that I love to have around moi.

This chapter is for laughter purposes, but individuals really do keep you on file. Laughing, but you think it is a game. There are so many of us who have not perfected in love yet.

**RESUME: JANE DOE**

janedoe@gmail.com

**MISSION**: To be in a relationship with a King who is stronger than myself, with no addiction, nor bad habits, a leader, provider, & protector. He opens my door and treats me like Queen at all times. Well, if he does not open the door it is ok. No big deal, but he has to treat me with the value that I deserve.

GREAT CHARACTERISTICS ! LOL!

- Bad Bitch (Laughing)
- Fun
- Go-getter
- Sweet if you don't rub me the wrong way
- Mean bitch sometimes, but only if you bring it out
- Hustler
- Love to hang with the bad bitches
- Cannot cook shit
- Club on the weekends

By the way this is not my resume, but this is the type of resumes females put on file, but look at her mission statement. She wants the world. And some man somewhere has her on file, because men really

## Hello, date a Boss.

like bad bitches who hang with other bad bitches. This is why men keep bad bitches on file, not for commitment purposes but his dumb ass feels like she is a challenge to him. Hello, date a Boss.

When I heard this I thought this was the funniest thing in the world but it made complete sense. But damn, men and women keep resumes on file. I feel like when you fucked up bad enough for it to be ended what would be the point of keeping that person on file. It is way deeper than keeping that person on file, this person has a piece of your soul that they are holding on to. It is up to you whether or not you pick that phone up or not.

This is intended for the humor alone, allow the universe to bring your soul mate to you. Stop with all the long list shit and treating relationships like a business transaction. There is nothing wrong with going after what you want, but don't get so carried away that you miss out on your dream guy or dream girl. And don't be so fucked up emotionally that when you do meet your dream guy or dream girl that you push their ass away.

# confession 6

## Love hurt like a motherfu*** but sometimes you just want what you want and when you want it. God help us all.

That was it for moi. When I think about love and the last time I felt it, knew it, craved it, this was it. I strived for the greatness part of moi all because someone who loved moi believed in moi. He took care of moi. He made me feel like a woman was supposed to. I never worried about were things going to get handled. I knew that they were. He had shown himself to moi repeatedly. When I think back on life I was completely clueless as to what it meant to love someone.

He also showed me a dark side that could not even get moi to stop caring for him, however it gave moi the strength to let him go. This was not love at all.

I became a woman that I never knew. I wanted to go back many days, but love had become the most painful place in my life that I had ever visited upon.

Some people say that love is supposed to hurt, well I completely disagree. How do I know, because when I had no clue of what it was it was taught to moi? Love is fun, engaging, filled with sharing with one another, it lacks fear, it is trusting, and it can't wait to spend time with you. This love that I experienced never hurt, used moi, called moi out of my name, nor did it disrespect moi ever. It just gave moi love. This was the love that God continued to give moi with no repentance.

At the end of the day that is all a woman ask for or needs, is love. She is created for this purpose to receive the beautiful gift of love. Often some men make the mistake to mistreat her to keep her from leaving. Playing mind tricks on your lady is never the way to go. This never works, she will stay with you but you will not keep her heart.

A woman will love a man forever when he gives her love. She knows that she should receive love, she desires love, and that she was created for it.

She does everything in her power to maintain the beautiful essence of it. Love is the truth. You may think that you don't want it. You may even think that it is your right to protect yourself from it, however real love will never hurt you. It will protect you, keep you safe, and you can trust in it with your whole heart.

# KNOW THE TRUTH ABOUT THE ROLLER COASTER RIDE LOVE WILL TAKE YOU ON

It so weird, I thought that I had it all together when I set out to write a relationship book. Well, at one point "Yes" I did, however along the way I guess I really didn't or maybe in my subconscious mind I needed to seek answers. Once you think about your life and the decisions that you are making, it does not really make any sense to you. What it boiled down to for moi was understanding what I didn't understand, being that I didn't get caught up in my emotions at all. If something happened to moi all I knew was to continue to move forward and move on. The thing that I did not realize was at the time-I was not dealing with things. I was instead just allowing them to sit there within moi. I heard so many times that I needed to learn how to love, but what did that mean? Who is to say what it is to love someone else? How could another person judge what is love to you? It made no sense, however it seemed as though I began losing the more I sought out to understand.

If someone would have told moi that they foresaw the hell that I was to come across in relationships I would not have believed it-not moi. The thing is that when we set our heart on a project, an idea, or a concept the universe sends us the experience needed to understand the fullness thereof.

I was soon to find myself crying, crying, crying, and becoming something that I normally wasn't a woman, filled with emotion, and a cry baby. This made moi think that I was being taught what this "Love" thing was that I had no clue of how to express.

Was I angry or void of understanding? I don't know what I felt, but I knew that I was feeling. I was not angry; however when I understood I became angry, it sounds weird but this is exactly how I felt. I made no sense at all to moi.

On top of that no one would say or reveal anything to help moi. This I hated. Is it wrong to use that word? I don't know but I did believe that when you accept how you feel that you are more apt to being open to love. Our feelings are relative no matter how others say that they aren't, at the end of the day we just want to be accepted for how we feel without someone saying that, *"It doesn't matter."* There are many things that we don't understand, but this is your journey so find it in your answers in your season.

As you are finding things out or are learning to know your partner you will also find out things about them that you despise, dislike, and detest.

You have to ask yourself, *"Why didn't we get to know that person more before you got attached to them in any type of way?"* There is a huge chance that you would not have stuck it out with them. It seems as though they feel as though you don't get them, and they definitely don't understand you. There are so many things that we do that we have no clue as to why we do them.

When we find out why it is often too late to fix things. Most times people just don't want to start over. You have to begin the process of learning someone new all over again. As hard as that may seem, as you get older you just get tired of the starting over game. It is all a process that if you don't learn to approach with a victorious attitude you will eventually lose. Take the time to learn yourself, become happy with who you are, or you will continue to just play yourself. We all approach relationships with different tactics. Here are some of the approaches that men have.

The different approaches that men tend to apply to get at females:

***Tactic #1* The boy approach.** They say and do mean things to get you to chase them. Remember this from the play ground, this does not work on any real woman. This is a game for boys and girls.

***Tactic #2* The, "*I am the man*" approach.** Everything that they say and do is revolved around the fact that they have not accomplished what they want to just yet, so they will do everything in their power to prove to you that they are the one for you. Every man in the universe has at least an ounce of this in his system.

***Tactic#3* The "I will love you" more than anyone approach.** He says that he will love you more than anyone that you have been with. He understands that you are a Queen. His goal is to teach you to respect what's real, because you have not received that yet from a man. Hmmm more than likely he is doing the same thing that the last guy that you dismissed did, thinking that he is doing something new.

He will be the sweetest man in the world, until he feels as though you are against him. WARNING! This guy can be just as spoiled as you are. Be careful, because two female spirits equal trouble. Women are emotional enough alone, when you introduce a man into the picture that possess the same emotions, well you might want to stop while you are ahead. All men have emotions, but when his emotions start to be exactly like his woman well there might be a problem.

He is strong as hell on the exterior but his interior well is a tad bit off of balance.

This man has an ego out of this world. He knows everything. He feels that there is nothing that you or anyone else can say to him that he does not know for himself.

The problem is you will have a hard time with him when he is not being Mr. Sweet guy, but all you remember is how sweet and great he is to you. He will do anything to satisfy you until he feels you are trying his manhood. If you desire to keep him, do not try him.

***Tactic # 4* This guy is the "Combination man," he is a combination of all tactics.** He has no clue what to do so he tries different tactics. This guy needs to find out who he is. He will slow you down. He is trying any way in the world to make it work, but his own unique way which is being himself.

Remember, You can never give a person that has never experienced having nothing to appreciate having someone who is of great value. He sees no value in nothing but himself, and you if you are willing to listen to everything that he tells you.

Women are natural born followers, however make sure that the male that you chose to follow is a great leader.

Last,

**Tactic #5 This man has no tactic.** He knows that he is a King. He has no need to defile you, speak down to you and he trust safely in God. This guy is Boaz. Ladies your probably have met him before. We let him escape, because we are still allowing a no good man to take his place.

Boaz is the man that has been watching you from afar. He can appreciate everything about you, while creating a desire for you to love and respect him all the more; for this very reason Ruth was willing to lay at his feet.

When we are not in a hurry to get a man or a woman we get the best from God. When we rush love we often end up with less than we are supposed to have. The first time I heard someone tell moi that God wanted moi to have a Boaz in my life, I went home, and I asked myself what exactly did Ruth do to obtain the attention of such man. As I studied I began to realize that a man of such character will find the greatest pleasure in a woman of such humility and understands the power of her servanthood.

Men like to be served. It is in a man's nature to be served by the woman that he gives his heart to. How can you better serve your guy?

1. Rub his feet after a long hard day of work.
2. Listen to his needs and how his day went.
3. Ask him if he needs anything.
4. Give him massages. Take care of his body. Treat his body as if it were your own.
5. Prepare and serve him his favorite meal.
6. Speak to him with kindness, men don't like to have to deal with a harsh woman. He has enough hard time in the world as it is, don't make things harder for him.
7. Give him your **trust**.

Of course you would have to know your guy personally to fulfill his specific needs and wants, the point is make sure that you are attentive to his needs. This could change everything for your relationship. Often times we focus on changing our partner when the focus should be on changing the way that we approach our partner.

# confession 7

## WHEN YOUR PARTNER PROVOKES YOU TO ANGER IT PUTS YOU IN A BAD ZONE

*"Love is slow to anger you but sometimes the wrong person can piss you the F off"*

There is nothing worse than living your life with someone that gets to know you so well that they are provoking you to anger, tears, and more pain than they are joy. For these reasons alone relationships suffer hard times. We all have deep embedded thoughts about relationships. In the movie (life story) of CoCo Chanel she spoke of her mother crying herself to her own death bed. Chanel watched her mother so often that she created her own perception of what a

**"Relationships aren't for me. I watched my mother cry to herself and she died alone."**
CoCo Chanel

relationship would be like from watching her parents. She decided that she wanted to take a different route.

*"Relationships aren't for me. I watched my mother cry to herself and she died alone."* CoCo Chanel

What good is it to have someone that you can't stand, that does not support you, and cares more about what you can do for them than what they can do for you. You feel worse with them than without them. You begin to feel that the entire relationship is pointless to even be in anymore.

On top of that, they never notice the great things about you. No one wants, nor desires to have a relationship with someone who they feel couldn't care less if you stayed, or care less if you go. These individuals don't even realize that they are this way because they have been cold for so long that at some point it just did not matter any more.

In the back of your mind you stay with them and stick it out just because you want answers. I began to wonder, *"Was I in certain situations in my life for love? When was the last time I had been in love for that matter?"*

Nothing made sense, besides moi writing, because I was sick of meeting men who were clueless how to listen, pay attention, or love moi. I was beginning to wonder what my own issues were. Sometimes the problem is the fact that we just need to evaluate our self, what we want out of a relationship, and our own intentions. The greatest relationships are the ones that are entered with a desire of nothing, but to love the other person. This creates a substantial amount of room for growth of both ends. It sets the platform for the two of you to win.

I couldn't for the life of moi understand why individuals stay in relationships that made them miserable; however I was determined to know. It could be that they have become use to the 'familiarity.'

The scary thing about being in a relationship with a partner who has an, I don't give a damn attitude, is that you begin to wonder who will?

Listen the worse thing that you can do is make the person that you love feel as though that you don't love them at all. It really destroys them on the inside. You don't want your partner to feel like being with them is a waste of time. No one human being likes to waste time.

In fact, individuals two main reason or excuse for something resulting in success or failure is either time or money. If you had more money, you would spend the time. If you had more time, you would spend money with the one in whom you love. The problem is that most people are lacking both.

A failed relationship is the direct results of not taking the time to spend with your partner. This is how you get to know them and begin to build with them. People spend more time with things, objects, smart devices, addictions than they do the people that they say that they love.

Making time for things all the time, will not get you anywhere when it comes to your relationship. Individual's who go into a relationship with a fearful attitude will hold on to the "I" instead of focusing on "we." It is easy for this personality type to live this way, because all they have to do is turn to the device that will never hurt them. Which one is it for you? I-pad, I-phone, or Apple laptop. Or do you just pull out your Beats headphones, turn up the music, and zone out?

"Relationships don't work, because people don't have the time."

You cannot build a nation, let alone the kingdom without caring for humanity. You and your partner need to practice this exercise for the next 3 days.

1. No speaking of I, more focus on us, we, as a team.

2. No electronics. Take a vacation together away from home. The house has too many distractions, it would be hard to make this work when you see things that need to be done.

3. Have a 'get to know one another' conversation. No arguing!

Talk – goddess
Listen – god
Talk – god
Listen – goddess

Talk – goddess

Listen - god

Complete this until the two of you have come to a mutual conclusion.

## DO NOT TALK OVER ONE ANOTHER, NOR ARGUE WITH THE GOAL OF GETTING THE LAST WORD.

It is time to find out why you are with this person. You will never build with your partner until you know that they are the only person in the world for you. All the time that you are spending with one another is a waste of time until the two of you reach a point of knowing that this is a person that you see yourself building with. You are going to waste time before you reach this point in your life. It is just life, it has nothing to do with the universe punishing you.

This is deal breaker for most couples. We live in a fast, microwave society where everyone is in a hurry.

"Pushing one another buttons will eventually kill whatever sparks that may or may not be there."

When you are being pushed to anger by your partner it is so important to know what is taking place. Your partner knows you better than most people do. In knowing your partner, you will also know how to push each others buttons. They will get a rise out of you, however do not retaliate, you are being pushed into the next dimension in your life. Nothing is as it seems and everything as you see it.

Pain will increase you and push you into your promise at the same time. Again this is why knowing why the two of you are together, it will change the way you respond to your partner. Whenever there is a purpose you treat the situation with an importance, with a delicacy like a flower.

People argue because they don't know how to take constructive criticism. When you learn the difference in your partner speaking to destroy you and your partner speaking to build you, there is a difference. It is all in learning.

*"The race is not given to the swift not the strong, but to the ones who endure until the end"* - God

## KNOW WHEN TO GIVE OUT YOUR LOVE AND WHEN TO HOLD IT

It took moi entirely too long to understand love and how you could love someone no matter what. I thought that people were stupid to love people past anything I still do in certain situations. Below are instances when you should love past and when not to.

You should love your partner past:

It is advisable to love your partner past their own mistakes as long as they are not bringing harm unto you.

1. A bad day
2. An attitude
3. Their trials
4. Their habits if it is not too horrid
5. The way that they look

6. What they have not yet found understanding of
7. Being a typical man, not listening to majority of the time, give him time to get this. He will.
8. Being a typical woman talking too much, give her time. She just wants to know that you are there and that you really love her. It is important to her.

You should not love your partner past CERTAIN things:

It is not advisable to love your partner past them bringing harm unto you.

1. Them physically hurting you
2. Them mentally abusing you
3. Any form of abuse

I am not suggesting for you to pick and choose when to distribute your love when you get ready. You don't want to distribute that love or being in love to someone who is not caring for it. It is like giving someone a luxury car for them to trash it. You would not do that, nor do you want to release something precious to someone who does not care for what you are releasing.

# confession 8
## STOP BEING A STATISTIC

*"I know that you don't want to rush and meet the family but do it anyway. Make sure that your future partner is not the seed of Chucky."*

It is beyond obvious that how you feel about certain things are as plain as day, but yet they still continue to do what you hate. Your partner knows that you hate it, however it does stop them from doing things that drive you crazy. You are the only person who can change that negative feeling of what you have allowed to be apart of your life. In life sometimes you will meet individuals that don't want to own up to their problems. Relationships are about sacrifice. This is something that people do for themselves to improve their own life, until they do this there is nothing that you can expect from the relationship.

The same problems that you had with your partner at the end of last year will be the same problem that you have next year, now is time for you to do something different for you. Prosperity comes through doing things in such a certain way. It is not a direct result of repeating old habits.

It is extremely important that before you get serious that you know the family of your partner. This will reveal their traits before you get a chance to see it in your partner.

My ex took me to meet his parents almost a year and half after we started dating, his parents fought, cursed, yelled, and damn near almost fought. This should have been a sign before I chose to get serious with him. The signs were screaming, "Hello, this is what you were in for." I fell for it. You cannot help who you love. Right? At least pay attention closely. Life will show you signs of things before they even happen. Don't be afraid of the sings.

Don't be afraid to meet your possible future partner's family, especially if you are a woman.

Women are entering into a new family not the other way around. Although both of you have to interact with one another's family for the most part ladies you are being lead by the ways of this man. Know what you are getting yourself in to. Some men are completely different from their families but they still carry similar traits due to their DNA.

Don't allow money nor his stability to make any decision for you, it is so important to know this man emotionally. Through knowing his emotions you are able to understand how he deals with different situations. It is only a myth that men are not emotional, however it is clear that they are. I meet someone who's family had a history of violence and abuse. As I said earlier in this book that he took great care of moi, inspired moi, and did things that made it hard for moi to ever leave. Sometimes we think men who are abusive that it is due to his financial struggle, but this male is insecure because of his DNA. It has noting to do with the woman. These men do such a well job of taking care of their women that it is least expected to come from them. These woman most often have no desire to be with anyone else but that one man. His goal is to make her feel inferior to superiority. Men are not the only ones who are abusive women have also become abusive to their male partner.

According to National Statistics, every 9 seconds in the US, a woman is assaulted or beaten. On an average, nearly 20 people per minute are physically abused by an intimate partner in the United States. During one year this equates to more than 10 million women and men. 1 in 3 woman and 1 in 4 men have been victims of some form of physical violence by an intimate partner in their lifetime. 1 in 7 women and 1 in 18 men have been stalked to the point in which they felt very fearful or believed that someone close to them would be harmed or killed. On a typical day, there are more than 20,000 phone calls placed to the domestic violence

## Stalkers in the US

**19.3 Million women and 5.1 million men in the United States have been stalked in their lifetime. 60.8% of female stalking victims and 43.5% men reported being stalked by a current or former intimate partner.**

hotlines nationwide. The presence of a gun in a domestic violence situation accounts for 15% of all violence crimes. Women of the ages 18 to 24 are the most commonly abused by an intimate partner. 19% of domestic violence involves a weapon. Domestic victimization is correlated with a higher rate of depression and suicidal behavior. Only 34% of people who are injured by an inmate partners receive medical care for their injuries.

This is emotional behavior that tells moi that not only men are emotional but women as well are using emotions to try and control something that they have no control over. None of us have the ability to control any human being. Deep down inside we know this and this is what causes rage: Knowing that we lack the power to control any if not every move of our partner. When you think like this or behave like this, love is usually absent from the relationship.

If you feel that you are in danger, please get out of the relationship immediately. Your life is more valuable to yourself first, know this. If you are in an abusive relationship please seek professional advice, help, or contact a hotline that is organized to assist you. Your life is far more valuable than receiving love from any other being. Love yourself first.

# confession 9

## LOVE YOURSELF FIRST

Love yourself first is the most important gift that God has given to you as a god and as a goddess, if you don't do this your life will be in chaos continuously. You have to at some point stop ripping and running for everyone else and find out what it is that will make you happy. We live in a world where everyone who is in it is looking out for themselves, which means that their motives have to constantly be examined.

When you learn to love yourself first, you will attract someone into your life that has the exact same love for self first. You can spend a substantial amount of your life pleasing everyone, but yourself. We enter into relationships with a spirit of unhappiness and we end up trying to find happiness from our partner. There is nothing your future partner can offer up to you or do if you don't have love and happiness for yourself.

Sometimes men and woman apply so much pressure to their partner to fix this, correct that, and figure out how to do this that it begins to weigh a toll on the relationship. The future goes from being bright to just being in a huge turmoil.

Having the freedom to just love yourself will decrease the amount of pain, anger, and violence that you experience in your life. All of these things are traits of self hate. The laws of attraction works whether you are putting positive thoughts out into the universe of negative thoughts out into the universe.

When I began to realize that I had more to learn about loving moi it was like I literally changed the way that I thought. My thinking began to transform, I began to meditate in order to complete and fulfill myself from within. The things that use to cause pain into my life began to cease from my life. I was starting to gain a freedom that was out of this world. It took so much time on my end to work towards regaining myself again.

We don't think about it sometimes but we give ourselves away every time we get in a relationship. When we have sex with our partner we give them apart of our soul, mind, and our spirit. If your partner is the wrong individual then you just released something of high value to that person. If this is the wrong person then they have also released some negative energy into your life. We are always in the presence of some form of energy. You cannot of course change anyones energy, it is something that must be done from within first.

I had no idea for years that I was suffering in situations all because the negative energy from the other person was allowed to have space in my life. The atmosphere, any form, and the people around you all make up this magnetic space that attracts more of itself into your life. The great thing is that when you love yourself you will begin to make up this space with the same love that you carry. This same love will exist in your space, in your environment, in your atmosphere, and in the people and things that are around you.

It is a hard pill to swallow to admit that you need to just love yourself. When this time came for moi to admit this in my life I did cry a lot, however a re-birth was taken place in my life. I closed myself away for a while just to rid my life of all negative energy. I began to notice that I was and could be more in control of life than what I have been. I started to verbalize, *"I am the one who is in control of my destiny, no one else."*

When you take charge over yourself it is so much easier when you face hard situations. I learned that getting upset was my worse enemy. Individuals who are not easy to anger are the ones who are more in control of what happens to their life. These individuals are more in control of their own successes, they are able to succeed more than the average person. To not get angry easily is to accept your god and goddess body in its fullness. The question is, *"Are you tired of living that old, yet negative life?"* These negative life forces have no control in your life, they have no door, and the only way for them to enter into your life is when you give them an open entrance.

As I learned the value of self, I learned that it was even more to learn. It was a Monday morning, I woke up, and called my mentor who was teaching moi a greater understanding of meditation. They shared with moi the things that I could do within myself alone, including increasing and decreasing my own energy, and bring myself back to a positive state of mental, spiritual, and physical awareness. He told moi that one day I would know the happiness of true love and that once I knew it that it would remain in my life for a lifetime. I trusted his words. He was releasing positive energy and positive thoughts about relationships in my life. Remember earlier in the book when I said that most of what we know of relationships is what we heard or saw as a child. Our perception of relationships are already deep embedded inside of us. What he did for moi was he changed the way that I viewed relationships. He changed my perception about relationships.

During this time of transformation, I also decided to do the 10 days to Success with Jack Canfield. This 10-Day Transformation exercise that help moi to see in its entirety that life was more about my response verses my reaction. Try it! It is completely free. There are so many tools that are out there waiting for us to use to increase our personal journey. This is also why I made a personal decision to take on clients as a life coach. After going through so much in my own personal life I decided that helping others means the world to moi. I pray that my journey gives you a greater sense of the importance of loving yourself first.

# confession 10

## SHE IS SPOILED, RICH, & FAMOUS

> "I am just saying, if both of you want your way the shit is not going to work. Relationships are about bringing joy to one another, but hey if you are spoiled then turn up with someone who does not mind letting you have your way." IJS

OK as if we care. We spend an entire lifetime of dealing with and taking bullshit from people since the day that we entered into the world. And now we are supposed to feel bad all because we are gorgeous, with positive energy, and the fact that we take the time to read to gain more intellect of self there is a problem. I mean men really need to learn a thing or two about being in a relationship with a woman who has it going on. Beautiful women have had to deal with so much from male insecurities, lack of understanding, and complaints. Men complain more than women sometimes and yet they don't want to hear our mouth. OK-whatever because I am beautiful, smart, & successful and if you don't like it then that is your problem not mine. Welcome to the world that I live in Spoiled, Rich, & Famous.

    It does not make sense, but when you try to live sensibly with someone that does not understand the power and importance of your indifference it makes things hard. The world is filled with all different types of personalities and being a spoiled brat is definitely one of them. Females who are spoiled develop these traits as a child, maybe from a father, mother, auntie, uncle, or the #1 spoiler Grandparents. Being spoiled is something that grows up with you. It is normal to be use to having things your way. You expect and desire more out of life. You have found pleasure in your desire of nice things, your family living in luxury is a priority. Your goal for your family is for them to have top of the line all of the time.

    The problem is that judgment of your spoiledness is right around the corner or maybe even in the same household. I say be yourself. It is a compilation of all differences that makes this world so incredibly special. Those who don't embrace their own difference just blend in the background. The background noise is usually everyone.

Stop judging spoiled babes. Rich men offer the world to a spoiled babe. However the world that he offers also comes with something attached. Hello! Women know that there is a price tag on everything. I think that we know this all to well, this is why woman have so much buying power.

**If the consumer economy had a sex, it would be female.**
Women drive 70-80% of all consumer purchasing, through a combination of they're buying power and influence. Influence means that even when a woman isn't paying for something herself, she is often the influence or veto vote behind someone else's purchase.
-Forbes

The thing is that a woman will go through hell and high water with a man, but why should she if she gets no love and respect for it. Saying,*"Baby thank you for being by my side, is not enough,"* but it does definitely help.

## WOMEN DESIRE WEALTH

When you love a woman there are certain things that you will do accordingly, including creating a plan of action, working to create wealth, & feeding yourself spiritually. Women were created to be taken care of, provided for, and protected. This is in all women. She desire that the person who is leading her knows where he is going. She can't help with his vision if he does not have one. There is nothing worse than feeding your woman a bunch of empty promises that you have no clue as to how you are going to fulfill them. In fact why wonder why she is always upset with you, tired of dealing with you, and wants to leave you the first chance that she gets. It is because you are constantly letting her down with your empty promises. There is one thing a woman hates worse and that is for you to tell her that you are going to do something and you never figure out how you are even going to do it. There are so many topics, subjects that will be touched on throughout this book, and some of it will sound straight crazy at first however we all know from experience that it is the type of shit that we all have dealt with or are dealing with currently.

This is one of the most difficult relationships to deal with, however it can be done. Remember that people attract who they are, so if you are spoiled then that is exactly who you will attract into your life. There are two of you in a relationship that are both spoiled, and both of you carry the determination to win. Both of you are and in the process of the two of you loosing one another unless you figure out how to win together as a team.

The two of you are in love, however you cannot help that you want your way, so your biggest fight is to find out how the two of you can get on the right path to get your way. Can we place a big #Control sign on your forehead? *"I want my way and I want it now!"* The two of you are talking, but in reality the two of you are trying to figure out how to still get your point across and get what you want. Does it work? Can it work? Will it work? Are you even worried about the questions? The truth is no you are not worried about answering any of these questions, because the only one that stands out is, *"How can I get my way?"*

So the two of you end up going your separate ways, however the two of you realize that it is the worse decision ever because in the midst of you wanting your way you realize that the other person is a part of you having your way. Now it is time the two of you to figure out how to remain spoil with another spoiled human being.

It is time that the two of you sit down and begin to talk about how to compromise not for your needs, but your partners. How can the two of you be happy living together and live the lifestyle of being spoiled? It is simple well only to the above average mind but you must get rich!

This is the only way for two spoiled people to be happy and fulfilled together. It sucks right? Well, not for two spoiled individuals, it is the ultimate, yet perfect plan. Sounds like the two of you have work to do. The following topics are topics based on the problems that spoiled individuals have. This is not for everyone only the spoiled shall survive.

**SPOILED & POUTING**

There is a use of the word "spoiledness" is this chapter and here out. Please keep in mind this word only exist in the mind of the most spoiled individuals.

The two of you are having a disagreement and it seems that there is no coming to terms about it. Now the two of your are pouting, the question is, "Who will give in first?" First one to give in will lose, most time this will be the woman. There is only so much a spoiled babe can take. In her pouting she will completely stop as she begins to ponder, *"How can I get things to go my way?"* She calls him up, *"We need to talk."* He responds, *"OK I agree."*

Although she has moved first, he has been waiting on it patiently. Spoiled men will exercise more patience than a spoiled woman. A spoiled woman's ultimate goal is to speed up the process of her spoiledness, so she sets out on a path to drive the greatest King that he can be out of him. In return he walks in his true path, while she enjoys even more of the fruit of her spoiledness.

Whenever someone is spoiled there will also be someone from your past competing with your present to spoil you more. Especially when him or her knows that you like being spoiled.

*"Hello, there has been way too much talk about you. You do see me over here complaining right?"*

Steve Harvey wrote the book, *'Think Like a Man, Act Like a Woman'* and he specifically spoke on the Momma's boy as one of the type of men that women date. When it comes to relationships often times our partner tends to turn to their mother. This is expected from any Momma's boy. It is cool however there are certain things that Momma will not do that wifey will. Momma will ride Daddy when he is not doing what he is supposed to. Although Momma is not saying anything to her child, because her responsibility is to support, nurture, and encourage you. Therefore she can see you lying around all day and never say anything to you, but let her spouse do the same thing she is going to say something. You cannot take advice from Mom unless you know that she is going to give you sound advice outside of her own personal emotions.

Things that Mom's do not like to do to their sons:

1. Put you out on the street. Although, it may be the very thing that will grow him up.
2. Let him go hungry. Although, he might figure out how to feed himself and his future family.
3. Let him suffer. Sometimes the first thing that Moms desire to do is bail their sons out of situations. Dads are different they want their sons to learn their lesson fast while avoiding making the same mistakes that they made with their own life.
4. Learn his own lessons. It is so easy for Mom to prevent her son from learning his lesson, Daddy wants his son to learn, but Mom stands in the way of his true guidance.

If you are dating a Momma's boy it can be a hard situation. But hey they exist and someone will date them, they are another personality type. Just know this up front that there can only be one Queen in a castle, so if you think that this is going to work just empty it out of your mind right now. You have to know what situations that you can deal with and what you cannot deal with. If you are cool with a shared position this will work for you, if not then let go, and keep moving forward with your life.

I am not anyones judge, but hey this is my book. I am not against anyone's mother, all that I am saying is that after you have done your job raising your son at some point you are going to have to trust what you have taught him or one day he may begin resenting you as their parent. Your desire should be for your son to be happy not getting in the way of his happiness. Majority of sons are just like daughters they chose a woman who has similar traits of their mother. Whereas daughters often chose men who carry similar traits of their father. My biological father was never in my life, in return I had to learn things the hard way.

When you do have a parent who is absent from your life and who was never involved this does not mean that you cannot have a successful relationship. And just because your parents hung in with their relationship does not mean that you will. You are going to have to learn to trust your own heart. Having the God giving ability to trust your heart will open the doors for you to build your own family. You may not want to start a family but you still want to allow room for your desires when it comes to matters of the heart to remain open.

If you are established and you have been living at home for years consider moving out to start your life. This could be a turn off to some females. Females can live at home and get away with it, because they can move from one covenant to another unless of course they are independent and desire to be alone. At the same time you have to check her motives. It should be the desire for any adult to be on their own. I could not live with my parents as an adult, because I know what that entails and I wouldn't be up for it. The truth is that we all dealt with rules as children because we had no choice, now that we have a choice you have to be the one who chooses wisely.

You can never expect a girl to do be a woman. You can never expect a boy to do a man's job. When a man says out of his mouth, *"I want to stay at home, because I am free there, and I don't have to pay any bills."* It is time to run like hell. He is basically telling you that he does not want to be accountable for anyone, including himself, & Momma's cool with the idea or she wouldn't be allowing him to do it right? So there are many problems in this situation with the son and with the Momma. You cannot help either one, because they are living the way that they are accustom to.

There are of course situations when a man or a woman has to go home, however the goal should be to be on your own, start your own family and build your own empire. A King will be completely uncomfortable living under his parents roof. His desire is always to establish his own and to build his own.

The greatest thing that you can learn from this situation is to move forward, because it is obvious that the Momma & the son are going through something that only the two of them can understand and they will take you with them before you know it. They are already believing that their way of life is right, they think that it is what God wants, and that is what they live. And maybe God does want it, everything in this life serves some form of purpose again the goal is to know what you desire for your own life.

God wants union, pure connection, peace, love, and not confusion. What needs to happen in this situation is the following:

1. You need to walk away if you are not happy.

2. Allow time for the two of them to find out on their own that their relationship is out of order for a mother and a son.

3. Accept the fact that this man is not lifetime material. He is only man enough for one woman, and that is his momma. Who in her eyes he is still a boy. Every individual who has a mother understands that no matter how old we all get that Mom will always see you as a child in her eyes.

4. Don't waste more time than you have to in this situation. This guy does not understand manhood, struggle, love, or responsibility. If he cares, he will not see it until you let him go, and he is on his own. Don't stand in his way, there is already enough of this in his life.

5. This guy is spoiled and he will suffer you for the rest of your life to listen to him pitch fits like a boy. You don't have time for this if your desire is to be settled with a man.

What this type of guy is good for doing?

1. Keeping you in stress. He is more to deal with than a teenager.

2. *"I am sorry. I am sorry. I am sorry," Are you tired of hearing this?*

3. This guy needs a woman with no goals, aspirations, and no responsibility. You can

never get this guy to understand you, again his Momma pays for him to live, party, and she pays for his bills.

    This guy is a dream jumper. He jumps from *"dream to dream"* every week, due to the lack of structure in his life. This guy can also be very much established. Moms if you are reading this guy cannot have a life, wife, or kids, due to the smothering of your love & guilt that is upon his life. He needs the room to not live in guilt. He needs the trust that he can make his own decision as well as be accountable for the decisions that he makes.

    4. This guy will create a life of inconsistency in your life, because of how he lives he will create the same inconsistency in the way that they think and feel in your life. If you want to go backwards in your life, family life, or career choices this guy will in fact take you on that ride. He will tell you that it is too much for him, all while living in the comfort of Momma's house believing that he is right and 100% man. He is a man but until he realizes that he has to cut the cord it will

always be between you are her. If she cares she will decide for him and let go. No woman wants a man to cut his mother off for her, nor does she want the pressure to feel like it is either Mom or her.

5. Wasting time. Don't allow this guy to steal your time, because years could go by and this guy will still be living the same way. You cannot change anyone, they are the way that they are until they see fit for a change.

Don't worry about losing this guy ladies, because there are no women lined up waiting for the opportunity to be with a man that lives like this unless she does not want better for herself.

Ladies you have told this guy the truth, he knows it, but Momma is not going to allow you to step in and have his heart. She is too busy manipulating him to do what her spouse should be doing. Momma's who are overly possessive over their son are either single or she is ignoring her husband, because somewhere she stopped trusting him with her heart so she began by giving it to a younger version of him the son. You see there is way too much destruction in place, and until this guy realize that he can't live like this there is nothing any woman can do.

Momma boys are sweet, they do not realize how they can make a woman feel when it comes to his relationship with his mother. This man loves his Momma, therefore he will love you however he will not love you the way that you deserve. His priorities will not be where they should be and he will continue to make his partner feel guilt for mentioning the obvious.

# confession 11

## FEELING FULL & EMPTY AT THE SAME TIME

The most difficult thing when it comes to relationships is dealing with yourself as a woman when it seems no one needs you anymore. This was a difficult phase in my life, in moi learning what it truly meant to have an intimate relationship. There I was fighting to be closer to the people that I love, while in return it seemed as though I was being rejected. By moi having this empty feeling on the inside it seemed like no one could see, nor understand how I was feeling. Maybe what I was experiencing was normal, however on the other hand I was so use to being needed it started to feel like I was screaming, "*Hey does anyone see moi over here?*"

The weird part about where I was in my life was the being full of purpose & empty of love. I could not explain it, nor my thoughts. I literally had no clue. Now all I had was the time to get myself together and it was the most confusing time in my life completely.

If someone would have told you what your life would be like, I don't think that I would have even believed it myself. We set goals for ourselves, our love life, and our families but when things come out completely opposite it can leave you in a state of confusion. And that is the last thing that you want out of life is to be confused about the life that you are living. A release needed to take place and an increase of understanding.

God was giving moi time to discover myself all over again. I was taking time to get to know who I was created to be in a new light. It was pulling moi out of my own self pity party. No one really wants to be in a pity party. It may seem like that, because we all know someone who has pity parties on a weekly basis and it is like Damn get over it. The truth is that some people don't know how to get over things, instead of them taking that first step and admitting that they need help they just continue to be alone and complain.

I use to complain, cry, and cry some more. I felt like I should not be going through anything in my life. I hated going through things in my life, however when I look back over my life I see the growth, and I acknowledge that I needed to transform from that bad place where I wanted others to feel what I was feeling. Learning that you do not need validation from anyone to move on with your life is the greatest feeling in the world. I learned that the only validation that I needed was the fact that God put a specific purpose inside of moi to live as a treasure here on earth.

The feelings that I use to feel concerning my life were negative, empty, and cold. I am glad that the spirit of God filled moi with his love.

Whenever you are feeling heavy and empty at the same time, please don't give up. You must know that there is work for you to do and the only way for it to begin is for your to heal. The empty feeling can be looked at as a void or it could be looked at as an empty space that is open and waiting to be filled with newness of life.

## IT IS TIME TO DISCOVER LOVE

"The moment when you realize that you don't know anything about loving someone outside of your own discovery."

The greatest lesson that you will ever learn is discovering that everyone loves differently. Learning that lesson is one difficult discovery in itself. A part of accepting and discovering love, we invest in everyone else, however we don't take enough time out of our day to invest into our own love life. Although we believe that our partners are supposed to just love us that is not the case. You must learn to love others by understanding how they love. It is not enough to stop at knowing yourself, you must go further and learn to love your partner the way they need to be love not how you want to love them.

As humans we walk around with filters and instead of learning to listen to our partner. The reason that we experience so much frustration is because we have not learned to listen to our "inner voice." What makes it even harder for us is realizing at such a later age in life that we have not discovered love.

Although we all feel like we know what loves is, it is only a mis-conception in most of our minds. Love is similar to success. There is only a small percentage of the world who achieves success due to their personal willingness. There are only a small percentage who achieve the powerful affects of love due to their willingness.

What is true love willing to do?

1. Quitting is not an option for those who truly love one another.
2. Understand what their partner is going through good and bad.
3. Willing to be a guide when their partner is in need.
4. To be a nurturing
5. It is protective
6. It helps you achieve your goals.
7. It has a spirit to be thankful.
8. It overlooks emotions to love with purity.
9. It stands the test of time.

10. It is charitable.
11. It thinks not of itself.
12. It operates in courage.
13. It deals with the bumps in the road along the way.
14. It works on improving until it is mutually achieved.
15. It has set a firm foundation to continue in love in the heart.

How many of us can say that we are operating in this willingness not just in our professional life but also our personal? If so, you are off to a great start. If not, work on being willing with the right one it will change your relationship. The two of you will begin to discover something new about one another. Every time the two of you walk into this new discovery it will renew your relationship.

# confession 12

## SUCCESS IN LOVE IS NEXT TO MONEY

"We are determined to learn, work, and build every area of our life, yet somehow we forgot to water our own garden at home. When is the last time you went out on a date with that special someone?

-Be bored for no one. Fight for your own success in love!

Success in a relationship is just as important as it is in any other area of your life. Although my life was not operating in the success of what it could be. Asking myself this very important question, *"How do I deal with the person in front of me?"* I know the thought may seemed to have an easy answer, however there is no easy route in love. It is similar to the journey of success, you hit bumps in the road, puddles, pot holes, but you must continue to travel. I wanted to know love in my life and essence of what it truly meant & what it could even become. I was wondering was I missing something outside myself or is it just something on the inside of moi that I was running from. Ultimately we don't want to feel like we are the problem let alone accept the fact that we are the problem. I can't help but to shout the word H-E-L-P.

Letting go is a huge part of the equation, however the real question at heart is *"What are we letting go of?"* Most times we let go of what we should be holding on to and holding on to what we should be letting go of. There are dangers in this life that can easily be a reflection of our own heart. Money is one of those problems and it always has been.

For many centuries money has been the foundational issue in homes across America. Relationships are torn apart because of the lack of financial education that individuals have. Which brings the thought back of wondering, *"Is love really enough?'*

If love is enough then how do we get past the thought of money? For the longest we are all told that in order for us to be successful at anything that we must know that what we desire is already ours, however this is easier said than done. The financial burden of money still sits on the head of the household to perform his duties and obligations to take care of his responsibilities. The same financial burden also interrupts the life of the woman who desires to make sure that all of the household needs are taken care of. The two of them with the burden get frustrated and it potentially causes the two of them to argue. And instead of them discussing how to handle their finances and take control over their financial future they remain quiet. They bury their problem with silence. They overdose the issue with no resolution.

In order for anything to work you must agree to make it work. Setting financial goals is a great start for change. Log online to **mint.com** this is a great site to start your financial planning. You are able to do the following:

1. Enter your income
2. Set a monthly budget

3. Find great investment tools
4. Savings tips
5. Tax tips
6. Set goals for buying a home, car, retirement, and kids college funds.

You must start somewhere to take control over your financial future. Start somewhere even if it is not here, sit down with your partner and get your financial house in order. Stop arguing and start planning together.

# confession 13

## FEMALE BOSSES WANT PARTNERSHIP

"When the two of you learn to operate in duality, you will also gain the ability to manifest all things."

Creating an equal level of partnership is what it takes to make it in a relationship. We give our partner what we want them to have and not what they deserve to receive. Being fair to your partner is something that you learn when you work towards gaining understanding of who they are. You can know your partner for many years and still be on a path of learning to understand their likes and dislikes.

An equal partnership is about becoming one, that means that you must take part of what you have + part of what they have= Oneness. When you can do this, your life will become in sync, and there will be harmony. Your goal is to flow into the next chapter, but *"How can you when the two of you are still not operating in equal understanding of the last chapter?"* When you decide to move forward from the last chapter, the spirit will deliver unto you the revelation that you both need.

Revelation releases so much wisdom unto people, that is why it is very important to grow together when you are both faced with adversity. When adversity hits, it will hit you with an equal portion therefore you must fight back with an equal portion of oneness.

## LAWS OF ATTRACTION

Accept the fact that people do what they want to do. You cannot change anyone, so accept that what they are showing you is what they want. They want someone to deal with them doing whatever they are doing. Individuals desire to be accepted for who they are not for who you want them to be.

Faith multiplied by faith will equal a double portion unto you. Operate in universal laws until you manifest them in its fullness. You cannot bypass that in which you need to operate in order for you to receive understanding. When the two of you gain understanding of the power of duality it will be life changing. There is so much power in the two of you coming together, this is fierce and it will not only strengthen your bond the two of you will become a huge success story.

All the two of you will be able to see and live is the fact that God has done something so unique between the two of you. When the two of you live in purpose and vision as one you will attract so much greatness into the lives of one another. The two of you will begin to enjoy a life together that most people only dream about. Once you have a plan, pray first, then pursue it. Prayer is our way of trusting God with the vision and plan that we have been given.

The two of you will be fought to come together, however when the two of you make up your mind there is nothing that the two of you could ever face that will be able to destroy your relationship. The greatness that the two of you will experience over and over again will be outstanding.

# confession 14
## STOP LIVING ON E

"The gas tank is not the only thing that can be on E sometimes you have nothing left to give the person that is sitting next to you"

It starts out all wonderful and glorious until you realize the person that you met is not the person that you met if you get what I am saying. The person that you are with seemed to have been just wonderful, but now that wonderful person seems to be just a nag that you wish would keep his or her opinion all to their selves. Well, that is how we feel and we are sticking to it right? Well, I am.

I had some horrible relationships and it seemed like the person that should have been the best thing to moi end up being the worse thing to moi. In my mind I could not figure out why or even how in the world did I end up with this person.

The truth is we do not know why we end up with the people that we end up with. All we know is that we did and that they sometimes became a horrid nightmare. Well, that is what I experienced. Accepting the fact that you have no clue of who you are supposed to be with and only God knows that would be a great start. Even looking inside yourself and saying maybe I could exercise the greatness of "patience." Yea why don't I just do that? I could not hurt any.

Besides the fact that I am fed up with people thinking that they can come into your life, do whatever they want to do and get away with it. I refuse to let that happen ever again. So what do you do next? Here is the kicker by the time you reach the person that God ordained, predestined or whatever you want to call it, you realize that you are on E. Yes, empty that is right and we all know what it is like to be on empty. When you are driving and your car is on empty, you are in a hurry, you have around 35 miles before your car just stops and quit on you. Instead of pulling over most of us just continue to drive. We ignore the obvious. I personally hate pumping gas.

This is exactly how we do our relationships. We are running on empty. We have been hurt and we have nothing left to give the person that God has desired to be in our lives. Instead of us stoping to deal with the issue we just keep going. You cannot rush love. You cannot place a time limit on it. You have to exercise patience with the person that you are with by first exercising it with yourself.

The 2nd factor to living on "E" is the fact that there is absolutely no "oil" in your car. We are not allowing the anointing of God to flow through us. We are not allowing God to work out all that pain. We can't expect the person that we are with to treat us right when we have not trusted a pure God to wash us clean. Allow God to cleanse you of your past. Your past does exist but leave it where it is. We even do this with arguments that we have. If you had an argument

3 weeks ago and another issue rises up don't bring it up, potentially it will just make the argument heavier. Yes, worse! Stop carrying that non-sense in your heart. When you ended the conversation you ended the issue. If something arises that is similar deal with that one issue, making it worse will not help the situation.

We hold on to pain like it is our prize possession. Learning to love your partner unconditionally will be the hardest task ever, but if you really love one another then you will make it happen. Like your parents, grandparents, and your children. Imagine what our life would be like if we loved the person that we were chosen to be we with unconditionally?

It is hard to realize what the two of you can become together if you don't realize what God can do through you alone. Each one of you should have a testimony to bring into the relationship, but how can you when you have not fully gave in to God's grace?

If we would give God the time, then we would also learn to give our partner time. We must learn to trust the spirit of God.

The 3rd factor is that while you are on "E" in a relationship that the two of you can now create your relationship to be whatever you want it to be.

Understand that while the two of you are on "E" that the two of you are also at a stand-still in your life.

*"It is time to silence the voice of frustration and embrace the voice of God."*

We complain, *"God I have been talking, yet receiving no answers from you. What is it that you want from moi?"* God is within us. He is in all of us. We have been given a divine purpose and now it is time to obey what that purpose is.

There are no accidents; everything is done with a divine purpose even the things that we disagree with.

# confession 15

## NOBODY WANTS TO LIVE WITH A VOID IN THEIR LIFE

"You will not be happy in a relationship until you are happy."

Mistake #1 We want our partner to fill a void that only God can heal and seal. We are often out of order when it comes to our desire. We must replace this void with God's will to fulfill the love that is within us first. How can you truly love your partner, when you have not yet become enough for you?

It makes no sense of the rules that we place into our relationship, let alone the expectations are so high that it is nearly impossible for any man or woman to even be there. In our mind we see perfection, which is not a bad objective to strive. However it is a goal that the two of you will one day reach, but for a moment let us strive to reach it within us first. Stop casting stones at others when you still have brokenness that is not even healed yet.

God wants to fill your heart with pure love. God's love cancels:

1. Fear
2. Doubt'
3. The fact that you don't trust your partner
4. Brokenness
5. Emptiness

Allow space for the spirit to just move frequently in your life and you will experience the ultimate love.

When you are being transitioned into a new place in your life, the hardest part of the process is when

God begins to transition you. You are being born again and that is exactly what it feels like. When you enter the world:

1. You enter not knowing anything
2. Not understanding anything
3. Not recognizing the people that you would normally recognize
4. God begins to literally strip you of what you know in exchange for who you really are

How do you make it through this transition, especially since you are use to being surrounded by so many people? There is life that is within you that is screaming to come out of your loins. The pressure is rubbing against your every side. As you begin to set your best foot forward to what you use to do, you realize that the old you has no place in you. However you are still *"feeling that void."* No one told us that maturing in God would mean being so uncomfortable but if you press through you will gain the understanding that you need.

You are probably wondering, what does the spirit of God want from us during this time. I don't think that God really wants something from us physically it just would not make sense. I do believe that he desire our wholeness because it makes the spirit within us operate in us naturally the way that it has been designed to operate.

1. God does desire our "healing" to take root.
2. God wants you to move on from your past.
3. The spirit wants the space to be pure and not filled with a whole lot of junk.

Stop holding on to old things, there is a new life desiring for your embrace. Love who you are. Love who your partner is. Love is the key. Love is the answer.

# confession 16

## QUEENS LOVE IT WHEN HER KING TAKES AUTHORITY

In a persistent effort to live this beautiful, fairy tale, love life that may or may not exist. You must strive all the way for it in your mind to live the royal life of Queens. Separating what you have been told with truthful knowledge of you and your position. Growing from a little girl and transitioning to a woman we often struggle with the transitioning of moving from the placement of "Princess" to "Queen."

A man cannot Queen you, unless you have stepped into the dimension of accepting the throne. Remember that some people are cool with being an asshole or a Bitch, especially if that is all that they know. Do not be conformed to anyone's way of doing things, especially if it is attempting to take you out of your own character. Queens exist in a category of their own and they are who they are. No Queen should have to explain her favor and reason for living a life of royalty, it is in her bloodline. If a man wants to be in a relationship with you, King has to be in his bloodline. Mixing oil and water is not the answer.

There is this huge mis-conception that we as humans feel that can potentially change other individuals, this has never worked for anyone. Change only occurs within a person when change is desired by them. Desire cannot be forced, it has to come from an individual's own free will.

We can all probably recall someone being in our life that you cared deeply for, however they completely screwed up the opportunity to be with you by desiring to change who you are more than accepting you for where you are. This is the worse thing that you can do to a person that you say that you love and it is completely unaccepted by a Queen.

Queens are chosen by God to live a life completely different from everyone else. She has to be accountable for this and whomever she is with has to be accountable for who she is.

Things that Queens Admire:

1. Godliness
2. Order
3. Substance
4. A man of power
5. Vison
6. Leadership
7. To be protected
8. To be understood and appreciated

At some point ladies as a Queen you must understand that you have several people who just want to hate on your position.

*"Never let your right hand know what your left hand is doing."* This is a quote that we all need to live by, because sometimes there are outside sources that are getting in the way of our greatness.

Some things are meant to be between you and God and between you are your partner until the right given season. There are wolves who are on stand by waiting to devour what you have been blessed with, this is why you must protect your position with the whole armor of God. Don't walk out of your home or your territory without your loins girded with strength and honor.

As you allow God to protect you, the spirit of God will lead your better half to also stay guarded to protect you. As a Queen you have to understand the importance of this so that you will only add value to your partner. Any partner that you are blessed with will understand the blessing of the value of where you are.

Queens are pre-filled with an understanding that their King will roar like a lion but protect them with all their might and all their power. She knows this and she is also prepared to protect this love, trust in this love, and believe in the greatness with everything in them together.

# confession 17

## *LADIES* GUYS LOVE IT WHEN YOU BUILD HIS KING'DOM

"There is a King inside of every Kingdom. There are multiple kingdoms you must know which one God gave to you. He is a great man, all you have to do is prophesy (speak) life to his already existing greatness"

Every man has the God given ability to become a King, however it takes his own desire + the right woman to come along to feed it. Out of the mouth of the wise, There are only a few things that a man really needs:

1. **To be fed.** A man needs you to be able to prepare him a meal in the natural and he needs you to also feed him with words that will build him spiritually.

2. **He needs intimacy.** Men are not like women. Apart of their success is them being able to experience intimacy with his Queen.

3. **He needs your heart to be sold out to his palace**. In the heart is where the chambers of his palace is. He needs to know that that place is for him and him alone.

It does not take as much to make a man happy as it does a woman, men look at the big picture, however women pay attention to the small details. These small details are what makes her happy. In order for you to be fulfilled ladies you have to learn how to build the man in whom God has blessed you with. There are things that your King deserves and you can be the only one who shows him that what you have is not available anywhere else.

4. **Serve him.** Don't make your man get up when he needs something to drink or something to eat while you are in the home. Serve him. In return he will take

you out and give you a break on occasion when you need a break. Serve him. Feed him. Cook for him.

5. **Set the environment**. Clean & burn scented candles. Kings want to walk in a peaceful, yet clean environment when they are home.

6. **Flirt with your King.** He knows that you love him, but remind him of how much you love him. In Return, your King is prepared to go to war for his Queen.

7. **Be his cheerleader, bouncy , bouncy!** Inspire and encourage him to keep pursuing is own greatness. In return you are able to sit and enjoy plentiful fruit with your King. Don't tear down your house ladies nor share your wealth with other women.

8. **Love your King** in a way that there is no need for no one else but you. **Respect your man.** He will honor, trust, and love you all the days of your life.

9. **Spend time with him doing the things that he loves.** Don't be selfish. In return he will want to know the desires of your heart.

At first this may seem a lot, however it must become your desire to make sure that the King, your King is taken care of.

# confession 18

## WOMEN LOVE MEN GUERILLA'S

*"A guerrilla does not overlook the small things. Touch her heart like no other man and you will always be her guerrilla"*

Guerilla's focus on the small things to accomplish one big objective. I know you see the big picture, however this is what will keep peace along the way. You want to keep your Queen happy, all while getting to the end of the matter. Men often times women will tell you that they are fed up with the small things that you are not doing. You respond to her, *"Why should it matter with all the big things that I am working towards.*" To her she wants to be a part of that and not left out of the picture.

She wants you to grab her with your confidence and caress her with all the small details that make up her day, her life, and her royal swag.

You have a responsibility to not make her happy, but to increase her happiness with fulfillment of your tender love for her and in return she gives you the ultimate respect as her King.

Protect her with your fearlessness. Keep her from the wickedness in this world. You will never see the President provide protection and shelter for himself without making sure that the first lady is given the same power, respect, security, and protection.

What does the first lady need?

1. Security
2. Protection
3. Respect
4. Power
5. Love
6. A platform to speak

He knows that the first lady has something to say, instead of bickering about it, he creates the platform for the people to listen to him through her. The world prefers to hear the voice of a woman. The world prefers to look at the woman. A King knows this. He prepares his life for her and his kingdom. He creates multiple outlets for all things to run successful. He has an answer for his Queen at all times. He leads her through the wilderness if needed. He makes sure that everyone knows that when they see Queen to not only listen to her, but to respect her. His presence lets everyone knows that sees her that she is the only one that he desires.

These are the same vibrations that she gives off. She is protective over what is hers and his at all time. She does not let up even when he is not thinking about it she is thinking protect what is hers.

# confession 19

## THE WORST MISTAKE IS TO CHOOSE YOUR PARTNER THEN ABANDON THEM

"The dumbest thing that you can say is that I did not know what I was getting myself into. People spend most go their lives getting to know themselves, when you meet the right one and you know that they are worth it take the time because if you keep walking away from that one person eventually it will become unrepairable."

When you are in a constant battle with leaving your partner eventually you begin to make the decision to leave or come back. You are creating the worse situation possible. Every time you leave them you are destroying trust, hope, faith, and the prosperity that could possibly flow between the two of you.

The movie Fireproof is a great example of what we are to exemplify in our relationship, although we cannot see the fire it still exist. Now the question is, *"Are you going to leave your partner?"* How many times have we abandon someone in whom we say that we love. Once you make that decision, be prepared for it to be harder to get into the heart of the other person.

Most of the time in relationships we don't fully value our partners while they are in our lives. We wait until it is over. I have never been this type of person. I will give my all until you give moi a reason not to. Somehow it seems that other individuals are backwards you have to earn their trust, they go into the relationship wrong off the rip. And by the time the other partner is fed up they want to work it out.

When you start in a new relationship go in with a full appreciation for the value of who that person is. Once you make a decision to walk away it is and will become very difficult to walk back. Most of the time this will end the relationship. Chose wisely! Chose wisely by knowing what you want!

# confession 20

## HOLD HER UP MEN AND WATCH HER MOVE YOUR VISION TO THE NATIONS

"Life is a game of chess, but a Queen knows how to move across the board."

This is a level in a relationship, but there is a higher position as a god or a goddess. When you embrace the god and goddess within you, all that you see will begin to manifest itself. This is what you want. You want to manifest what you have seen in the spiritual realm into the physical realm.

Guys when you share you vision with a woman of purpose, it becomes her priority to manifest your seeds of greatness. A woman of purpose was created for this very reason. A man of vision can only survive with a woman of purpose. This is God designed. Trust and know that she has you. She is your help meet. Get behind her and watch the magic unfold like never before.

Men if she shows you signs of power, get behind her she is going to deliver your greatness into the earth. The world will know who you are. She will make sure that the world knows you.

# confession 21
## *B*E PREPARED FOR KARMA

"Karma is not just a bitch, karma can also be a blessing. It just depends on what you put out into the universe."

# confession 22

## ADDICTS HAVE DESTRUCTIVE HABITS

*"To be honest yes, if they show their ass the first two years, please know that is who they are. Don't waste time with someone who has no value for yours."*

You can learn a lot from a person within 2 years of your life and you must ask yourself these important questions:

1. Have I wasted my time?

2. Can I afford to spend more time with this person?

3. If I move on will I just be starting the cycle all again?

4. Are you happy with the steps that they have taken to make your relationship the best that it can be?

5. Have you been the only one that compromises in the relationship?

6. Do they have add problems that you cannot foresee yourself living with for the rest of your life? You must answer this question, because they may or may not stop the problems and this is something that you must be ready for.

Sometimes one of the biggest problems is an addiction to something that is more to them than the relationship. It is not an easy task to deal with people with addictions.

Addictions:
A. Come before the other partner
B. Are distractions
C. Will cause you to lose energy
D. Will challenge your life for the worse

It is time to ask yourself these questions concerning dealing with people with addictions. This also has a great deal to do with the "Law of Karma." People who are addicted to something will release those same vibrations into your atmosphere.

1. Are they willing to get help?
2. Do they acknowledge that they have a problem?
3. Do they realize the fact that they are losing you behind their addiction?
4. Do they care? Or are they saying, "This is me, deal with it, because I am not changing?" There is no desire there for the other person to get better or for them to even improve the relationship.

This is one of the most challenging situations to deal with in a relationship, because no matter how hard you try nothing that you do seems to be enough for the other person. Then there is the issue of the fact that it is taking forever for you to reach a level of fulfillment in your relationship. You will eventually face the toughest decision of your life:

1. You will either face walking away from them.
2. You will make the decision to love them through it.
3. You will accept the fact that love is all you can offer this person and that their change must come from them realizing that they are destroying their selves and not you.

All of your decisions are hard, but the best one that you have to make is "accepting" what they are refusing to accept for them the truth that there is a problem that is deeply buried inside that only they have the power to fix.

I wish there was something or even one thing that could be given to help aid with the pain that the person without the addiction has to deal with. Most often the person with the addiction is not feeling what they are taking the other person through. This is even harder to deal with, since you want that person to understand how you feel. At this point of their addiction how you feel is completely irrelevant. I am sure that at some point in all of our lives we have watched a love one self destruct with an addiction of some type. It is hard to watch and you will have to make a tough decision.

Although you want to be there for the person with the addiction you must learn to help them and stop badgering them. Ask yourself:

1. How can I show them love that it seems as though they don't even deserve right now?
2. Why I am looking at my pain instead of how much pain is buried in them?

You see up to this point everyone has been screaming to them that they need to stop. You love this person, but *"How can you show them that love right now?"* I understand that you feel like if you back off that they will continue to do the same thing and not change, but how will you know if you refuse to do it?"

One day they will begin to wonder in all their hurtful acts, *"Why does this person continue to show moi love?"* Real love is not about your feelings. It is about showing forth an action to release something even greater into the person that you love.

You are agreeing to make a commitment the moment that you fall in love with them to empower them with God's love not your idea of love. Can you say, *"We all have issues, some are greater than others, but at the end of the day we all have them."* Once you realize that someone has loved you past your issues, then you can also love someone else past their issues.

I wish there was an easier way to love. I am not suggesting that love is pain that is not what I believe. I do believe that love is acting in compassion, understanding, a sound mind, and wisdom even when it makes absolutely no sense to you.

I do not believe in anyone being in a situation of danger or an environment that they don't feel comfortable in. I for one would not do it. I would however love that person from a distance.

When pain comes look at the situation in a positive light and deliver your greatness.

# confession 23

## KNOW WHAT YOU ARE IN FOR

"If majority of their family is filled with drama and somewhat nuts, you might want to pay attention when you see the BS. The worse mistake that I ever made was to not pay attention."

Meeting your partners family can be nerve wrecking especially for the Mom meeting the female. Mothers and Fathers both judge from different perspectives.

1. Mothers judge the woman that their son loves based on how many characteristics that are similar to hers.

2. Fathers well they don't have that judgment if she looks good and can cook he is all for it.

Then there is that point where the relationship begins to get more serious, now everyone is learning one another, but there are also disagreeing with one another. This is the phase where the ugly side begins to show itself in everyone. Don't worry you will get past it when you realize that you have one common interest love. Once you realize that all of you are in a room centralized around love it changes your entire perspective. Then you realize this is why he loves her, this is also why he loves them, and then all the other minor details become irrelevant at that point.

If the man feels like his Mom is way too much she will be the last one that you meet out of the family. If your guy is a Momma's boy his Mom will be the first one that you meet.

I don't have too much experience with my Father giving a guy a hard time and scaring the shit out of him so he knows not to fuck with moi the wrong way. I didn't have the pleasure of the experience. I think that all females should honor the fathers that are in your life that protected, cared for, and loved you.

When you are in a relationship the families matter to a certain extent. We all love our families even with the craziness and all the drama. That is just the way that we are. We love our family unconditionally.

I really want to move into talking about the fun stuff. Come with moi to the next chapter.

# confession 24

## YOU ARE A COUGAR & IT IS DRIVING YOU CRAZY

*"You have hit your prime and your hormones are going crazy, but so is dealing with his young ass. Ladies mature faster than men do therefore this will only be a headache. But hey some headaches are worth it."*

When you first heard the term 'cougar' women were at least 45 and older, but now you are a 'cougar' if you are 7 – 10 years apart in age. He might be 23 while you are 38 years of age. This sounds great, but there a whole lot of problems. And no this is not my age. Stop guessing! Lol!

1. Men mature at a slower rate than women
2. There is a huge lack of understanding between the two of them
3. You are still not where you want to be and you spend most of your time fighting with the spirit

of what you have already lived, because he or she wants to be free to party, hang out, or get sloppy drunk. You on the other hand have out grown that phase in your life. Time out for the foolishness right.

When there is an age difference, there will be some challenges to overcome in this area. Often when you are in a relationship with someone who is older they will tend to want to teach you to catch up. This is difficult, because the other person feels as though that you are trying to change them.

There is an age difference that we have acknowledgement of, however that is not the true issue just like the fact that you are of a different race, culture, and sex. The problem is reaching a level of communication that consists of the same knowledge, wisdom, & understanding. This is what most couples go to war over. You love one another, but you don't understand what in the hell the other person is speaking about. Take the time to invite quality into you love life, show some respect for your partners needs.

If you are a cougar and you are dating a younger guy, don't plan to get serious place it in the category where it belongs sex.

# confession 25

## TEACH YOUR KIDS RIGHT & THEY WILL SET THE STANDARDS FOR YOU

> "When your daughter just stands at the door of the car waiting for your potential guy to open the door for her she is just setting the standards high. A great father will teach his daughters how he wants them to be treated. A great mother will teach her sons how she wants them to be treated. The standards that they set they also desire you to have."

As you are sitting in the car with your potential partner, your daughter refuse to move from her seat until the door is opened for her. She is saying through her actions, "My Mom has been through enough, she deserves the best, and someone needs to teach you, so I will show you."

Kids have no filter, they say, speak, do, and ask for whatever they want. I don't suggest bringing this potential partner around unless you plan on being serious with this person. Children get just as attached to a relationship as an adult does, sometimes we don't recognize this but they do fall in love just as you do.

We must explain, explain, and explain things to them so they understand that even when a relationship does not work that it was not their fault. This is important, you will be surprised of how many children blame themselves for break ups.

Children are funny, because they often say what we are thinking out loud.

1. Hmm, Do you have a job?
2. Where do you work?
3. How long have you been working there?
4. Did you go to college?
5. May I have some money for the movies?
6. What did you buy me?

As you saw in "Are we there yet," in the movie her children were setting the standard for their Mom. When children blow off that person or show no interest, ask no question, and are not involved with your this person, they are showing how they feel, and how this person acts towards them. Children are like mirrors they show a reflection of what they are feeling. All you have to do is pay attention to their actions.

If you are to get into a relationship with someone who has children, please know that you have to get to know them as well. It is a package deal or stay out of all of their lives. This is critical if you don't believe that you can handle the worse of a situation, don't get in it period. It is very harmful to every party involved.

# confession 26

## *F*ORGET THE RESTRICTIONS THAT YOU HAVE ALLOWED OTHERS TO PLACE ON YOU

As much as you would like to make others happy, you must first take the time to learn what makes you happy. Don't wake up just to find yourself missing time, energy, and serval pieces of your puzzle that has not even been put together. In the real world a puzzle is a game where the person putting it together will exercise your mental energy, however your life is a puzzle that must be put together by you.

Some people are meant to find happiness with others, but when your purpose is higher, *"You will only find loneliness in what others find happiness in."* It was so weird to me, but it seemed as though something was literally wrong with me. I could not find happiness in what seemed to be normal to majority of the world. It felt more like loneliness. When you are out of your element, away from people who are opposite of you, this feeling is normal. We find happiness in being ourselves and being surrounded by people who are walking in similar purpose.

Nevertheless feeling this way is normal for peculiar people. We live in a world that insists on telling us that something is wrong with us for being different, for standing out, or for embracing that peculiar purpose. This is why our relationships fail you have one peculiar person and one normal person who flows with the rest of the world. In the long run it does not work out, because one of you will eventually give up self to fulfill the other one in order to have oneness. It does not matter which one of you makes this decision it will still end up in a failed relationship. It is unfair for one person to be happy, while their partner is in misery.

Relationships work when two people are both of, "peculiar spirits" or both are of "normal spirits."

Peculiar people must be dealt with in a certain way. Example, You look up into the sky during the night and you will see only a few stars out, those few stars represent the peculiar people while the dark space represents the rest of the world. Although we need both for the universe to exist, for darkness does not exist without light and light does not exist without darkness. Even if it is for a season to be with someone, know its purpose, and move on. It is not meant for us to stay with some people forever. Learn to let go when it is time and hold on when it is time.

# confession 27
## *DON'T* BE FOOLED, WHAT YOU SEE IS WHAT YOU GET

"It is what it is"

**I**f you think that people will change just because they are in a relationship with you this is a mistake. People are who they want to be and you are no different. People change, grow up, and mature when they get ready to not when you want them to. The question is, *"Can you deal with what you see or is it a deal breaker?"* You must ask yourself this and then you must answer this question, no one likes to waste time.

If you know that you cannot deal with a person for the rest of your life, you are only wasting time. You must also ask yourself the question, *"Why are you still holding on to a relationship that makes your unhappy?"* You know when you are not being fulfilled, as well you know what makes you feel like you can continue to move forward in a relationship.

As humans we make the horrible mistake of holding on to people who don't even come close to fulfilling your love life. The worse part of it is that you are the one who allowed them to occupy a space that possibly another person could come in and complete your love life.

We are not speaking in the terms of you not being fulfilled within yourself, we are speaking in terms of you being able to share and receive that love in a relationship.

## WHAT IS THE POINT IF YOU ARE NOT GOING TO LISTEN

People all over the universe need to practice the "*Art of Listening,*" this would change relationships as we know it.

## DON'T ALLOW NEGATIVE ENERGY TO INVADE YOUR SPACE COUNT IT ALL JOY

# confession 28
## WE DON'T CARE, MAKE UP YOUR MIND

The hardest thing for couples who are in relationships to do is for them to listen, not only to words, but brokenness, silence, body language, frustration, what makes them happy, listening to what makes them sad.

Listening to your partner is a form of art, and the only way for you to perform is listen to all that makes up their space. You must learn to be creative when you're in a relationship or it gets boring, and when you are bored you will eventually lose interest. There goes another failed relationship. In order to correct failure you must learn how to be successful at something, this means that you must turn to your inner person. The ways to love is within you. You are the only person in this world that you are in control of, once you know this you will allow the spirit of freedom and peace to just flow in abundance. The best relationship that you can have is the one that you have with yourself first.

People desire a relationship, but they don't want to put the effort in when things are going horrible. Some of the worst things teach you how people feel about you and for you. No one wants to be in a long term relationship with someone who constantly takes you through the changes of being double minded in the relationship. It is not enough being good enough for your partner on one day and not good enough on the next day.

Growing up I saw my Grandmother and Grandfather love each other constantly even when it seems as though they could not stand one another. I remember saying to myself, "I want to be just like my Grandmother when I get older, but I forgot to say God give moi a man that is just like my Grandfather." Someone with the potential to become greatness, not someone who will think and believe that their way is the only way.

God has a way that is true, loving, and kind. When you are heart broken from loving someone, it will be mended.

Love is something that does the following:
- Covers a multitude of sin
- It is not judgmental
- It does not point out all your faults
- Forgiving
- Grateful
- Trusting
- Willing
- Has a spirit to up lift one another

When it comes to relationships all we ever desire is some form of consistency. Some people switch up their ways every chance that they get. It is hard to trust people like that, you never know what they want and desire. The goal is to grow with someone.

# confession 29

## FEMALES LIKE TO PLAY HOUSE

### THE LUXURY OF PLAYING HOUSE

# Case Study : Barbie vs Goddess

i dream big but only those BARBIE dolls get moi

*"We grow up thinking that our lives will be perfect. The perfect house, the perfect couple, the perfect spouse, the perfect kids, and 2-3 cars parked in the driveway. This is how I became the #fairytaleprincess Lol! #noworries but somehow this #lifestyle is now for sale on social media in fact I just saw the perfect little family and everyone in the pic is smiling."*

If you don't dream big, there are no worries I have had this under wraps since a little girl. I never wanted a small doll house. *"Momma get moi the biggest one that you can find."* I was a big dreamer as a little girl and it never changed, my dreams just got bigger.

This is my confession #29 I had to earn this level of joy the hard way. The first magic spell that was ever cast into my life was through the fairytale beauty of the doll who went by the name of Barbie. Each Barbie had its own special magic that came in the form of something so simple that I wanted every Barbie that came out. This was preparing moi to live a life where I would never be satisfied with myself. Barbie was always changing something about herself and she became a new Barbie every time she made that change. Barbie was magically putting the thought into my mind to nag a man for every small thing and to notice every little thing even if it destroyed something great. Barbie magically was releasing a spirit, an energy to little girls all over the world that no matter how pretty she is that it would never be enough. Her slim figure small waist, skin complexion, pink lipstick, full head of hair, fashionable outfit, and high heels. Lets not forget that she had Ken, one of the cutest men who there were not many of. Ken was few. There were probably 10 Barbies to come out for every one Ken.

Parents help their children grow up into a false reality all because they are not paying attention to the subliminal messages that something as simple as Barbie and Ken dolls were putting out. From the time of our childhood we are all being brainwashed to live an unhealthy life that does not consist of love but lust. We are taught to lust after things in a constant motion. We are taught that nothing that we do is ever good enough. As children we sit in front of a television that is also teaching us to lust, and live in the idea of playing house instead of building from a solid foundation.

When we get older we are not mentally prepared to live in reality, because everything that we have seen in our subconscious mind has shown us something so different that we are unable to cope with the smallest things. It was not just Barbies, it was also cars. Every new hot wheel that came out, a little boy all over the world wanted one. The hot wheels were magically teaching the little boys that this is what would make him cool and desired by women even if he would potentially attract women who would lust after what he could give them verses the love that would possibly be in his heart.

    We grow up with stupid ideas that skin color releases some type of special power into our lives, somewhere this idea was learned from something that was teaching you how to lust verses love. In return many adults pass down this same spirit to their child and when their child learns this hate and the fact that their skin color makes them no greater than anyone they are set up for more pain. These are all taught behaviors. To tell a child that their skin will cause hatred releases hate into their lives, this thought begins to develop in them, and they begin to go throughout life carrying this idea.

    Hatred is a mean spirit that comes from the heart of individuals who walk in hatred. If you were ever hated on it is so much easier for you to pick up this spirit without even knowing that you have it.

    Love is blind, means that love does not look on the outer it looks on the inner, at the heart, and at the spirit of that being. These ideas of love must perish before they destroy all of humanity.

We may desire a white house, a white picket fence, 2.5 children, 2 nice cars, and a hard working man but make sure that the desire is not from something that has put a magic spell on you. There is nothing wrong with having these things, just make sure that it is right for you and that you are not trying to keep up with the idea of playing house with someone. Hard times will hit, and when they do you it will reveal whom you have in your life. When the love is real, a hard time will only make the bond that the two of you share even stronger not weaker.

*Little girls are taught to want things, material things, pretty things, things on the outside, and there is no genuine desire to want to build with anyone for who they are verses for what they have.*

We get fed the luxury of playing house at an early age, as little girls we dress our Barbies up, put them in a huge doll house that consists of upstairs, downstairs, huge bedroom, and closets filled with clothes, shoes, and jewelry. Not to mention that outside is parked our convertible cars. Meanwhile there is nothing in the picture that is insinuating that it would be a great idea to be in love with yourself or the man in your future. *Little girls are taught to want things, material things, pretty things, things on the outside, and there is no genuine desire to want to build with anyone for who they are verses for what they have.* This hurts later on in life really hard. I was this little girl obsessed with every little new detail of Barbie.

Barbie's are marketed to little girls between the ages of 3 - 11. The doll was inspired by a Lilli doll that was known as a sexy novelly gift for men, which was based on a popular comic strip. The doll was developed by a woman named Ruth Handler in the 1950s. This was amazingly surprising due to the fact that Barbie was 5'9 weighing only 110 pounds, the complete opposite of Ruth who was short, with short hair, and a very confident woman. However she created a doll that would create low self esteem, eating disorders, poor mental health, and body image issues.

Research shows that little girls who played with Barbies would later have eating disorders between the ages of 12 - 25 years of age. "Women stated that they played with Barbies before they were diagnosed with eating disorders. Research also stated that 18 out of 25 women who played with Barbies at a young age would prefer to be run over by a truck verses gaining any type of weight. The research also shows that the girls who viewed the Barbie doll reported lower self esteem, and a stronger desire to be thin. The Barbie doll has become many things to little girls including a mentor, a role model, and someone that the little girls would admire."

In the 1960s Ruth introduced a new doll "The Slumber Party Barbie."

Including: View the image below:
1. Diet Book
2. A scale
3. A hairbrush
4. A sign that said, "How to lose weight? Don't eat" (Slumber 1)

In addition to this the scale only went up to 110 lbs, even to this day women all over the world fear standing on the scale. Something so simple as the toys that little girls play with can mess up their entire identity without them even knowing it. When little girls are so young they are so impressionable to be influenced by many things from televisions, ads, and their toys just for them to later to desire plastic surgery, bigger boobs, bigger lips, smaller waist, and more height.

The only thing that can be done to stop this is for more parents to become spiritually aware of what their children are playing with and that is difficult in the society that we live in.

The little girl who plays with Barbie becomes a woman one day who is either weight conscious, plastic, and they have a heart that some man will have a hard time understanding because he has no clue as to how long subconsciously things have been playing on her mind. When she looks at him and suggests that she needs to lose weight or that she has been thinking about getting a boob job he looks at her like, "Why?" He looks at her through the eyes of perfection, but she is still viewing herself in comparison of Barbie.

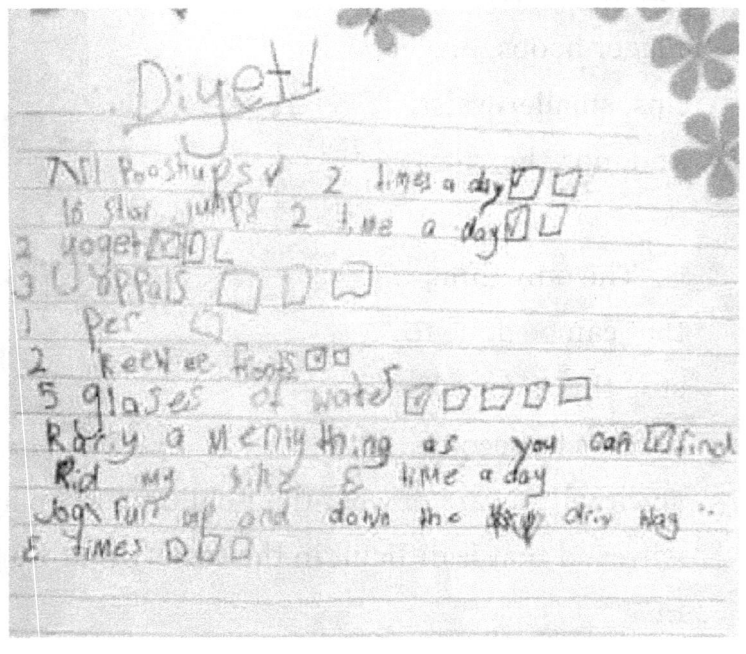

In my research that I found this article that was so sad, because a mom had made a post of something that she found that her little 7 year old girl had written down. This diet {diyet} really upset her that her little girl would have this type of pressure at such an early age to be thin and concerned about her looks. This is not to say that Barbie is to blame, however little girls all over the world aspire to be like Barbie when they are little.

If you are reading this and you are living under the pressures of todays world or images placed in your head as a child say out loud, "I am beautiful just the way that I am!"

On the other end little boys are subconsciously preparing for war playing with their army men and guns, fighting with the little soldiers on the battlefield insisting that going to war is the reason they are bold, courageous, ready, and willing to go to war to protect out country.

All of this explains why little girls ask little boys to play house with them and little boys still want to play with their army men. Men are less likely to make a commitment that females are because it was

The above note was found by the Mom of a 7 year old little.

not embedded in their minds subconsciously like it was for the little girls.

It is so important that we watch what goes into the subconscious mind of daughters and sons. We all get older with issues that are more than likely hard to shake.

# confession 30
## GIRLS ARE SMARTER THAN BOYS

Is it just a myth. No, females are smarter than males. We have different instincts, whereas boys look more at simplicity. Females desire to know more than males do. We have this instinct this is why a woman can be in the worse situation and figure out how to get out of it. Her mind is instantly on a rampage of thinking of ways to improve herself and the things around her. It is a God given talent.

The thing is that you are fighting over who is right and who is wrong. Him or her? How do you deal with the bulk of this information to move forward in success concerning your relationship? The two of you are fighting on a regular basis, and all you know to do is to argue concerning the difference of what the two of you know, how you were raised, what you understand, and what you don't know about one another.

What would happen if we were to view our relationships like our business? Applying time, effort, positive energy, and relationship building to move forward in prosperity, as the two of you sit down to reach a level of understanding you must reach a "level of listening" first. You cannot know your partner if you refuse to listen to them. This is one of the most important steps that should be practiced on a daily basis.

Once you learn to listen, then allow the gender to not even be a factor. If she is stronger at handling something let her. If he is stronger at handling something let him. She is a woman. He is a man. Stop fighting over your roles and just get it done.

# confession 31

## LADIES KNOW GUYS MORE THAN THEY ARE GIVEN CREDIT FOR

"Ladies know just about everything, if man would ever listen."

Men are so simple that they are complicated; they act upon things that make completely no sense to us at all. While we are at home worrying about them, wondering who they are with they are off majority of the time working, contemplating, and planning to give you a greater life than you already have.

I was able to see for myself men hard at work, on the clock away from their lady while being completely frustrated about the fact that they are away from

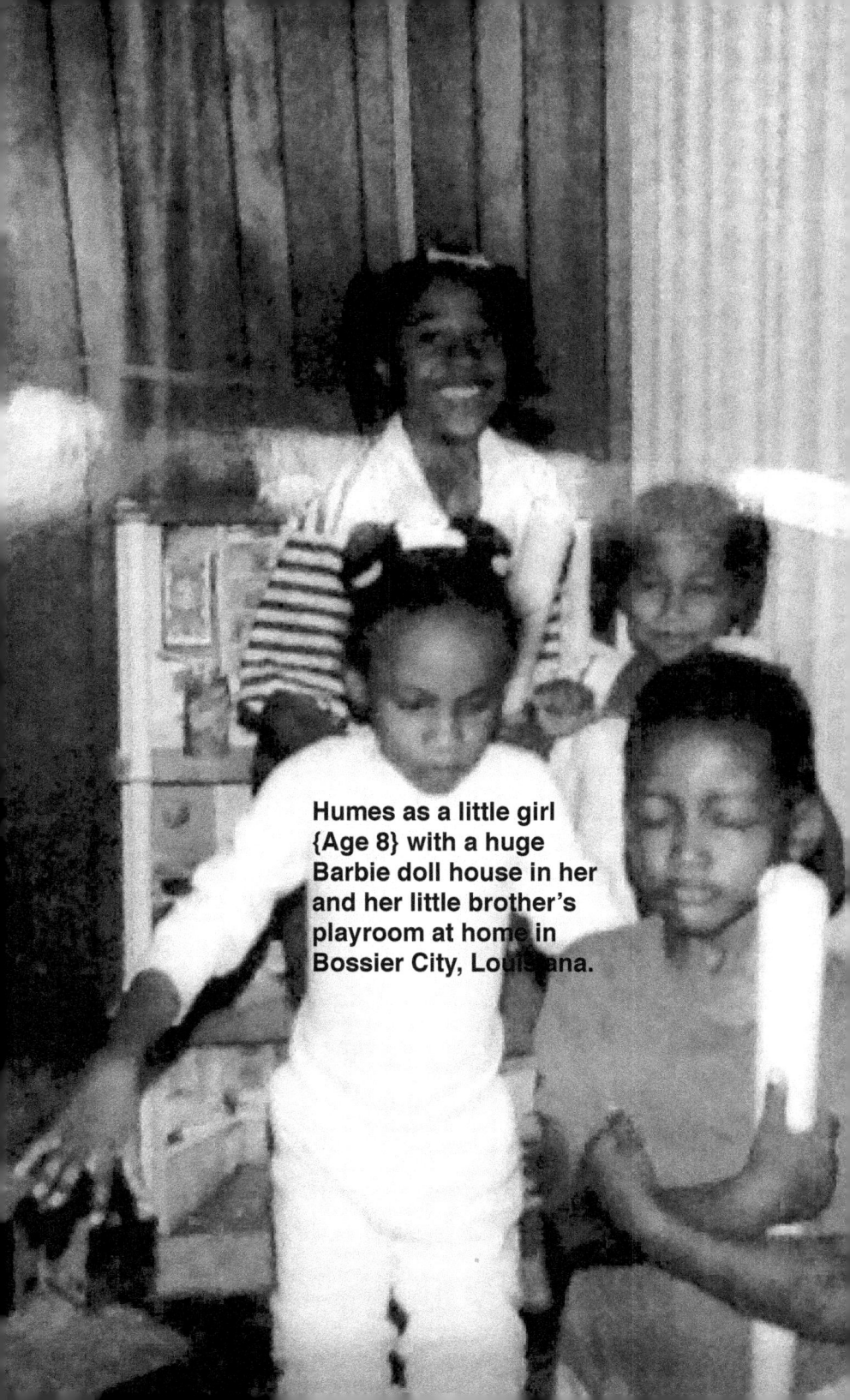

Humes as a little girl {Age 8} with a huge Barbie doll house in her and her little brother's playroom at home in Bossier City, Louisiana.

them. It makes no sense, however I was able to hear a man say, *"I am tired of all this and all I want to do is go home to my lady. She is waiting on me."* During the same time I was taking note. There is so much that goes on with men that women are clueless of. Most often they are just trying to survive and make a way to take care of you and their responsibility. In return they come home to a billion questions, because they forget to tell you what they were doing. Men don't always think about what they are doing like woman do. We cannot expect a man to think like a woman. I know that Steve Harvey told all of you to Think Like a Man, in return women expect men to think like a woman. It is not going to happen. Men are men for a reason. Women are women for a reason. When wisdom takes effect in the life of a man or a woman it is because they chose that they are ready to receive it.

I remember my brother told moi that most of the time men know that their woman is right they just don't want to admit to it or they are not ready to accept what they are saying. He also said the best way to know if a man is telling you the truth is he will respond to certain questions with a question. He will not give you a direct response. This is a sign that he does not want to share something with you concerning what you are talking about or he wishes to avoid the conversation all together. Whereas woman just ask questions just because they think way too much.

    Men don't realize that woman just want to be reassured about life, where the two of them are going, and that they can remain confident in the direction that they are being led in.

# confession 32

## MYTH ABOUT WOMEN

"It is only a myth that a real woman desires to be with a rich man. Real women love real men, not rich men. Any man can get rich as well as any woman."

Most women go after men who are rich, who drive nice cars, and have a fat bank account. #Myth Most women know that men who have all the money and material possessions are less likely to fulfill them in a relationship, more likely to just have them as a trophy, and less likely to care about anything they think or have to say. We are dealing with myths concerning what real women are really thinking.

Real women go after real men, which means that it is not about any of those things. It is about the heart, soul, and integrity of that man.

When you believe in God there is no need to need others for anything. Your relationship with God must be straight first and foremost in order for you and your relationship to be successful.

# confession 33

## HE IS YOUR god, *HE* IS A PROTECTOR

"Every woman wants to be protected by her man"

We all have seen this at some point whether it is happening for you or you are passing it by. I saw a couple walking along side of the road. A car is coming their way and the guy grabs his lady, pulls her out of the way gently, and then he switches positions with her. He chose to stand in the way of any possible accident or anything that could possibly cause hurt unto her. This is the sign of your "protector." He does, acts, and thinks with the same mannerism as God would with you and he allows it to manifest into your life in the form of man.

It is a more than awesome characteristic when you find out the man that you care about cares about God. He will speak and act in the position to be more than you need him to be without you even speaking it to him. You have to trust him to live in the power of the free will. Free will was given unto us all for important reasons:

1. When we say that we love God he knows it through our action(s) and our freedom of making any decision.

2. When our partners has free will and they choose to stick it out good & bad.

3. When our children who have free will say that they want to spend time with us, not always money.

4. When options are no longer options and they become our way of living.

A god acts totally different from a King, his attitude, his persona, and his confidence is way through the roof. He is fearless. He is powerful. He maintains his position. He is the only being in this entire universe that can handle his goddess.

If you have been blessed with one of these precious jewels from God, serve him, cater to his needs, and give unto him sexual fulfillment. He deserves the ultimate pleasure.

# confession 34

## SOMETIMES OBJECTS RULE YOUR LOVE

*"Everything you see in the physical world is only an illusion of the truth"*

It is extremely a very dangerous thing when you hear the person that you love helped you out, nevertheless you made them angry enough to say, "Bring my S**t back." When you hear this please know that you partner is about to use what they are helping you with to now control your every move. It is a very evil spirit and knowing this will save you time, money, heart ache, and pain.

Whether you are male or female you can pray against this spirit, however the first thing that you want to do is for you to accept the fact that it is nothing more than an evil spirit. Relationships fail since individuals want to keep their evil spirits and maintain having a desire for material possession alone.

If your main goal is to acquire a bunch of material possessions then you have already lost at love. Love is so much more than a car, clothes, and a new house. Love has the power to gain and obtain whatever it wants, but if the spirit between the two of you is not right then it will not last.

Ladies I know that you want him to cake you up, all women want a man that will do for her freely, but it is rare that you will find a man that will do for you without wanting something in return. When you don't put out, he won't give out.

Sometimes you are blessed enough to meet a man that straight up believes in the vision that God has given you. Men desire to know how you are, how you respond to situations, what your weakness are, and they want to know your strengths.

The biggest exaggeration a man can ever tell is that he is giving you 100%, because if what he is giving you now is 100% then there is no room to grow, nor to gain understanding to achieving more. In his mind giving 100% just means that he is giving his all, however I don't believe that any of us give our relationships 100%.

Sometimes we overcompensate for what we are missing that is why 100% makes sense to moi, there has been many times that I felt like I was giving my all without receiving it in return. It makes you feel unappreciated.

The truth is that everyone needs someone, none of us were put here to be alone all of the time.

When a man is rich he also desires to be in control, when you share an issue that you may have with him he loses it and takes it as , *"Don't be with me then."* He does not know how to deal with things on a personal level and as long as he is alone he does not have to. He enjoys things and as long as he has his things, toys, etc…there is no real need for you. This is why when he is not around you he still shows no real need to be around you. To him he is the same way all the time, however to his woman she desires for him to open up to her.

There is so much these two can do together, but first they need to move the mountains that stand between them. If you can't help your partner get through a hard time in their life, vise versa then the reason the two of you are together becomes questionable.

Take some time to talk without getting offended all the time. An offended man or woman is a sign of brokenness and insecurities. We all have them, we just need to acknowledge them and heal those wounds.

Know that this guy is not a bad guy at all, but if he has taken time to come at you then he is going to take just as long to give you 100%. To know him is to love him. He gets better with time, that is how he operates.

A one on one conversation between the two of you will sky rocket your relationship. According to Gary Chapman or The Five Love Languages, "Quality Conversation" could help a great deal.

*Like words of affirmation, the language of quality time also has many dialects. One of the most common dialects is that of a quality conversation. By quality conversation, I mean sympathetic dialogue where two individuals are sharing their experiences, thoughts, feelings, and desires in a friend, uninterrupted context. He goes on to say if your partners primary love language is quality time, such dialogue is crucial to his or her emotional sense of being loved.*

There should be a genuine desire to sympathize and understand your partner thoughts, feelings, and concerns. Most often we badger our partners instead of taking the time to understand where they are coming from. We end conversations without ever hearing what the real problem was, because we are so busy to get our point across. We often become mean through yelling, and saying harsh words not caring that we are adding to the hurt or issue that is already existing. Instead of solving that issue we potentially create another one. Actions like this damage relationships in the long run. Behaving like children to hurt someone in whom you feel is hurting you only because you are not healed of your previous hurt does nothing for the success of the relationship.

If couples knew the intent of the person that loves them, they would never get angry however instead of looking at the intent they run emotionally on how what is being said is making them feel. This person may be a words of affirmation {Love Language} If they are you must be careful on what you speak to them, they are not built for anything outside of language that builds them up.

Just remember that through taking the time to learn one another you also learn to stop taking offense, and the two of you begin to build a strong love bond in your relationship.

# confession 35

## *B*RIDLE YOUR TONGUE, IT CAN BE DANGEROUS

> "The tongue can speak you into more trouble that a little bit. Learn to close your mouth when you are upset, and practice patience not anger, for anger is only a thief of blessings, love, and time.

You can literally kill the greatest experience in your life with an awesome person simply through speaking positive words of affirmations regardless of what you see being produced out of your partners life. This is one of the most difficult challenges that we face in a relationship, having the ability to hold dear to the words of the living truth even in the weakest moments of your life. When you harm the person in whom that you say you love, it may become very damaging to them therefore you want to exercise patience, wisdom,

& knowledge in living in the truth. Today marks a great day as you begin to speak as you read, *I will not turn back to a life that was filled with lies, lack of knowledge, wisdom, and understanding. Today marks the best of the rest of my life, because that is all God sees in moi when he pushes moi to move forward.*

Even if you have to bite your tongue, surrendering to a powerless moment is not worth it. You will only live in the regret of what you said from that point on.

God is calling you to fulfill the greatest part of your life and all you have to do is surrender to the greatest part of who you are. There is no turning back! You will not regret giving your life to love. It is harmless, fruitful, and the greatest gift that you will ever give in to. If you think about all the hell that you have experienced you will also know that majority of that experience has come from your tongue.

Your tongue has formed mountains, pillars, rivers, valleys, storms, dead places, hunger, disasters, blessings, and curses all out of the same body. One body embodies many members. You must be wise when you are releasing your many members to work on your behalf to ensure that you form a bond of unity, love, and pureness.

When a relationship is on its last leg, even if there is hope to rekindle the fire you pour water on it instead of throwing wood in the flames. How can a fire continue to burn if the work in which you began you stopped? You have given up. Quit! There is no life in this. I have realized that there is no life in quitting. You shall not have success when you accept to fail. Again what you speak will determine your next days, weeks, months, years, and lifetime of love.

You are not bound to what you have never spoken, however if you spoke it you are therefore also bound to manifest it unto your life. The best life is the one lived with a well kept tongue. Evil shall no longer roll off of it. You will no longer give in to the worse, in return you shall have the best of the greatest kingdom living that one can experience.

Individuals all over the world look to have an "experience." Whether it is sitting in Starbucks with a cup of that great coffee or shopping with one of your close friends. All desire to have an experience and we have been taught to walk into an experience that has already been created. What needs to happen is you need to "create an experience" for yourself. When all is said in done, your life will be just as you want it, how you want it, and it will be experienced with greatness that is beyond measure.

# confession 36

## YOU WERE CHOSEN BEFORE THE APPROACH

> "So you really think that he just checked you out? I am going to let you have that."

Women you are already chosen by man before you even approach him. Every man has an idea of the woman that he wants, needs, and that can help him through his hardest phase in his life. He wants a woman who is not looking at his circumstance whether he is poor, middle class, or rich. They all desire the same certain thing of a woman.

I was on the phone with a friend of mine in the year of 2014 as he began to tell me what all men desired. His exact words were, "Future made it clear." My responses, "What?" He said, "Trophy! Every many wants a trophy on his side, but when you add intelligence, a mind for business, a woman who walks in purpose, and a woman that is carefree. That is what a man wants. That is a total package, even if man can only have some of that he wants it."

Men are different from women. It may seem like they just want to try things, however men are very cautious about trying anything new at all. A man will walk into a room filled with women and pick out the one that stands out most to him. He will go the distance of talking around her to just get to her. His goal is to get to this one woman. If he truly values her, he will take his time even years before he ever approaches her, this is why women are more heart broken than men are. Women are in more of a hurry than most men, their clock is ticking. Women are ready to tie the knot and most often they miss out because Mr. Perfect is already apart of her life but she does not notice him due to him not being ready to reveal himself.

This is why when you finally meet Mr. Right he says, *"I have always wanted to talk to you. You were always special to me. I didn't want to risk losing that."* All he is saying is that he is careful with your heart and if the opportunity presented itself he would be the one in whom would do right by it.

Guys who are in just a quick of hurry as women are, sorry but usually are not the right ones. They are put in the thirsty category. It is not that a women will not date you, but why are you so quick? Women eventually take you for a guy who wants anyone. They eventually don't trust you. Please understand that there are some women who see longevity with you and they are asking questions to bring clarity but deep down inside even if a woman gets serious with you she knows that you are not serious material even if she choses to settle for you. Women are like this, they give up hope, they weigh their options. They try hard to make worthless situations work. It is in the DNA of women, this is why they are naturally mothers. They see potential everywhere. The thing is potential is nothing without action.

Be patient, love does not exist without it. Men and women there is someone for you. Ladies the guy that is supposed to have you has already chosen you. Spend time with God and when he is ready to take it there, he will let you know that you have been "Chosen before the Approach."

# confession 37

## *LEAVE THE PAST WHERE IT IS*

*"The past is dead. It no longer exists, you cannot go back to it. Stop talking about it to your future partner. If your partner is great, just accept your future right now where God blessed you with him or her."*

Now when you hear the truth there is no way that you can deny it, especially when it is coming from a man, who knows other men, and converse with other men about relationships.

You can never carry dead things, situations, nor people into your future. The worse thing that you can do when you enter a relationship is to bring up your partners past without their permission. Majority of the times the other person does not want to speak on the things that are irrelevant to his or her future. "I know what you did last summer." So what! It is no longer here. You cannot bring it back, therefore why take something dead and attempt to bring life to it?

Speaking of the past is a bad habit that is filled with curses, besides who needs or wants reminders of where they no longer are. Thank God I am not where I use to be!

# confession 38

## *T*HERE ARE LEVELS TO THIS SHIT

"Levels are about climbing in an upward motion, if your partner is not up to it then push forward without them."

Whomever reaches the level of faith first, partner mount up with the wings of an eagle, your life depends on it. The most difficult opposition is when your partner reaches greater levels spiritually, naturally, mentally, and physically. This has become a challenge all over the world for couples.

Who is on who's level? Is this the question? The two of you have been dating for a while then that thought appears in the mind of only one, *"He or she is not on my level. I can do better than this."* Once you have this thought everything is pretty much downhill from that point.

Levels are like great experiences that you can only experience when you are experiencing that level. You may want to change the level that your partner or date is on, however that decision can only be made by that person. Understanding this saves the two of you time. Knowing who you are is very important to having a great relationship. When you know your limits, you walk in with appreciation and understanding from the beginning. Although learning one another is a process, you can still go into the situation with what you know.

There are 3 important things that you can take from this entire book and it will help you to embrace the love from within.

1. Know God
2. Know yourself
3. Love who you are

It is that simple, but so many of us avoid this. We have taught ourselves that it is much easier to avoid things than to grow and to accept things for what they are. Above are 3 important things to know but they are also 3 important levels that you must embrace first before you can even think of loving anyone.

# confession 39

## LAWS OF LOVE & RA'SPECT

"Everyone has a certain level of love and ra'spect for their parents even if they have never been in their life."

I Love you Dad even if you have never been apart of my life

## THIS CHAPTER INCLUDES AN EXCLUSIVE INTERVIEW WITH THE ADVERTISING ARTIST ROBERT JONES

It is imperative that we do not confuse what is being the head & the body. As we begin to flow in the orthodox order of greatness. God is the head of all. Man is head of woman. The body receives whatever the head partakes in. Now here is the challenge naturally male and female both have a head and a body, both also manifest entirely two different roles, nevertheless the day that they join God says for them to become (one). This must be one of the most difficult things to do since the number (two) represents also duality. As man screams, *"Respect moi woman!"* Woman screams, *"I wish you would just love moi."*

Let us look at this same aspect from a royalty perspective as the man becomes King and she becomes Queen. A King releases 50% authority to his Queen to make decisions as he would, in this situations what Queen says goes & her King trust, love, and honors her enough to back it. King has also released half unto Queen. They are one, due to his position also as head he has now released half of him to the body. In this understanding what is (two) now becomes (one) through the knowledge of order.

When you read my book, "Submission," (I will release this in the future) you will read deeply into what we all fight about whether male or female there is literally a war going on the inside of us fighting with:

1. The laws of leadership
2. The laws of love
3. The laws of respect

Men desire respect period! We need to stop bitching about non-sense to them ladies.

EXAMPLE: WHY DO YOU KEEP LEAVING THE TOILET SEAT UP? YOU ARE JUST NAGGING HIM

Ladies stop being so unfair to men nagging them because they refuse to let the toilet seat down when they left out of the bathroom. He had to lift it up when he went in because you left it down. He is doing the same action that you are doing when you are leaving the bathroom. We must learn to be fair to our men and give them the respect that they deserve and need. We must stop badgering them about every little thing because they are giving us the same respect in return. Think about it if a man said something to you at every little thing that you did it would drive you nuts so shut and respect him as the King of your castle. Majority of the flow of your greatness will flow from respecting what God has blessed you with.

We cannot experience any of the greatness that God has bestowed upon us until we realize that we are both through freedom called to submit to the greatness that both partners have been gifted with.

We all have a gift from God that is both spiritual and natural.

## WATCH YOUR RESPONSE

The easiest, most weakest response to your partner is to respond in anger, speaking curse words, yelling, physical abuse, and control. These are quick routes to disaster. When you respond to your partner in this way all that you are doing is turning a great situation into a bad situation quickly. Once you have released the evil you cannot take it back, therefore you must learn to exercise patience, virtue, love, humility, and remove the spirit of pride completely.

When you read my bio you will read about some of the abuse that I experience & of how far back it goes. It is a spirit that is embedded in you from the time that it starts. It could be verbal abuse in your childhood, however if it is not dealt with it, it matures into physical abuse in your adulthood.

Abuse creates the atmosphere for so many things to go wrong in your life:

1. Depression

2. Anxiety

3. Frustration

4. Low tolerance of being able to contend with difficulties with day to day task

5. Low self esteem

I realized that as I spent more time learning, developing self, and focusing on what would create growth for moi that I was not as bad off as those who could not even wake up to face their own heart ache.

As you take a self assessment look at all the factors that are binding you from your future. Get to the root and pull it out where it started or it will continue to fester within you.

What you are about to experience is a miracle of understanding. As I stood, looking at books in Books-A-Million thinking that maybe my relationship life would possibly be better if I knew my Father.

As I stood in thought, an older gentleman asks, *"Are you all right young lady?"*

My response, *"Yes I am all right. I am only thinking."*

He replies, *"Well it seems as though something is wrong & I have been known to help others. Everything happens for a reason."*

At the moment I thought it to be strange that he was talking to moi. However I did respond, *"Yes, I believe and know that. I was just thinking about writing a relationship book, however I was also thinking about the relationship that I never had with my biological father. I was thinking maybe I could interview some different individuals, with different cultural backgrounds for the book."*

His response, *"Let's go."*

*"No offense Sir, but I don't know you."*

His response, *"Yeah I know, however lets go to the front of the book store. You can interview me."*

I thought strange. *"What is your name?"*

He replies, *"Robert Jones."*

Now the craziest part of this conversation was the fact that I was seeking answer of my father, who's biological name is "Robert Jones." God you are hilarious, this is a joke right. It has to be, well I thought anyway. Since I knew that this was a major sign from God, I continued to start the interview and "No" this guy is not my father.

INTERVIEW

**DATE:** APRIL 19, 2013
**INTERVIEWER:** MONI'SOI HUMES
**INTERVIEWEE:** ROBERT JONES
**OCCUPATION:** ARTIST {ADVERTISING}

**Q. WHAT IS IT LIKE BEING SUCCESSFUL AND HAVING A PERSONAL LIFE?**

A. Wonderful, it is a matter of choice and I chose this passion. I am thankful to God for the courage to trust him, myself 100% without worrying about the naysayers. I am committed to my heart desires. Most people change their mind like the wind and yet they wonder why they are not successful.

Staying in even when it flip flops, that is all a part of life. (Tenacity) Stick to it regardless. It is the only way to understand the fullness of what it is all about.

**Q. WHAT HAS BEEN THE BIGGEST SACRIFICE THAT YOU FEEL YOU HAD TO**

**MAKE CONCERNING YOUR CAREER? AND DO YOU FEEL AS THOUGH IT HAS AFFECTED YOUR PERSONAL LIFE IN ANY WAY?**

He paused for a second...

So....You don't feel as though it has affected your personal life in any way?

Of course, but how else would you know? You will always wonder would of, could of, should of, and never did anything for anyone. It is what people say when they don't have the courage to follow their dream.

**Q. MOST PEOPLE DON'T KNOW HOW TO HANDLE THE STRESS OF SUCCESS AND MAINTAINING A PERSONAL LIFE, IS THERE ANYTHING IN PARTICULAR THAT YOU HAVE DONE, ANY TIPS THAT HAS HELPED YOU TO MAINTAIN YOUR PEACE THROUGH YOUR ACHIEVEMENTS PERSONALLY?**

I have kept God as my partner. My one true love, that I can truly depend on.

My response,
Basically it is your relationship with God that gives you peace in the midst of it all.

## Q. WHAT IS YOUR RELATIONSHIP OR HAVING A RELATIONSHIP WITH GOD LIKE OR WOULD YOU SAY THAT YOU ARE A RELIGIOUS PERSON IN ANY WAY?

My relationship with God has nothing to do with religion. It has to do with the confidence of knowing someone loves you without guessing, "Do they really love you?"

My response....
You seem like a strong believer, who is very confident.

## Q. HOW DID YOU GET INTO THIS PLACE? AND WHAT ADVICE DO YOU HAVE FOR THOSE WHO LACK THE SAME TYPE OF CONFIDENCE TO HOLD ON WHEN IT SEEMS

**LIKE THE BEST AND A VERY EASY THING IS LETTING GO?**

**A.** The key is to know that it is not a feeling.

My response...

**WHAT DO YOU MEAN BY THAT?**

There is an assurance when you know that you have the right thing to win. It has been proven to you often and it leaves you with no doubt in your heart. How can you not be assured, therefore you would be bold as a lion, you walk with confidence?

**Q. HAS THERE EVER BEEN A MOMENT IN YOUR LIFE THAT YOU FELT LIKE YOU JUST WANTED TO LET GO, BUT DIDN'T? HAVE YOU ALWAYS BEEN THIS STRONG? COULD YOU PLEASE ELABORATE?**

There was a brief moment of silence from Mr. Jones...

A. Usually, "No," because I know myself, but in people, "Yes." Everyone goes through that. It is how you look at it. You must change your thoughts. When you shift your thoughts you shift your situations.

For example...

Someone could look at a pair of shoes and complain. They look so old and dirty that they just don't seem to be in style.

Then along comes a stranger who looks at the same pair of shoes with cold web feet thinking that God answered their prayers and will love those same shoes truly and wear them with confidence and pride.

My response....

Very deep, however could you please explain further that in which you spoke?

Mr. Jones response...

The answer is within the parable. One person thought about the style, but yet another looked at the blessing and saw the true purpose for those shoes.

My thoughts...

At this point my mind began thinking of how much we over look, because we are looking at the wrong people and the wrong places, when we should be focused on fulfilling purpose. I was looking for my Father to answer moi. God was speaking to my spirit at this point, *"Stop seeking for the truth and let the truth find you."* In Books-A-Million I met Robert Jones, a different one, who had the answers. "Begin with God."

Mr. Jones says, *"It is all about God's love. Love in which you are truly looking for. Your father was probably looking for the same thing, but he was looking at the style or he was looking for a different reason. He was not looking for the true purpose."*

**Q. IS THERE ANYTHING ELSE THAT YOU WOULD LIKE TO ADD? I KNOW THAT YOU ARE AN ARTIST AND THAT IS A REFLECTION OF YOUR RELATIONSHIP WITH GOD?**

**A.** That is a reflection of a relationship with myself.

My response, I have never really heard it in that sense, what exactly do you mean? A reflection of yourself, what exactly do you mean?

**A.** In order to be true to someone else you must really be true to yourself. He nodded, "Yes." I mean my heart is me. It is all different formalities, techniques, ideas that are required to create a piece of art. It is really letting the inside of you come out. A form of self expression, you feel more alive, more relaxed, more you...

I would say that I have found happiness within moi. This is where it truly lies, no money, no car, no house, no thing. The kingdom of God is within. He asked me if I had a stepfather. I replied, "Yes." He said, but you always wanted your biological father that is how a woman learns to treat her man.

My response, that is funny that you would say that, because I spoke with some Jehovah witness and it became a debate about the kingdom of God being within.

Mr. Jones, *That is their opinion. Look back at the parable.*

Thank you!

**Q. FOR SOME REASON I KEEP THINKING ABOUT THE WORD "SURRENDER" IN WHAT WAYS HAVE YOU APPLIED THIS TO YOUR PERSONAL LIFE AND HOW CAN OTHERS APPLY IT TO THEIRS?**

**A.** Surrender to what?

My response, How did you surrender to your purpose?

**A.** I was little kid, around 4 or 5. I use to get a whooping everyday for doing something. Whatever it was I don't know but whatever it was I use to get in line. One day my mom had a switch in her hand. She had all my siblings lined up and she asked us all a question. We had to answer or else we would get a whooping with that switch. When it was my turn, I still remembered when she asked me the question. I said, "Momma----I want to do something with the brush." Then my older siblings knew what I was talking about they knew what it was. They knew that I wanted to draw. I was afraid but my Momma switch went down. I thought whoah! I don't have to sleep on my stomach tonight.

Do you get it? Do you know how dramatic that was for a 4 year old kid. It was so strong that I remembered even until this day.

**Q. So you would say that at that moment that you "surrendered" to who you are."**

**A.** Yes, and it has been a blessing in my life as well as others and I am truly blessed.

Can you see that me at 4 years of age. My parents use to plait the switches. They would hurt.

**QUESTION FROM MR. ROBERT JONES- WHEN IS THE LAST TIME THAT YOU HAVE BEEN IN LOVE?**

It is about being honest with yourself. People are scared of their self and that is who they fear the most.

You are afraid of yourself

I was thinking in my head that I was the one doing the interview.

My response....
Why do you feel like I am like that?

Mr. Jones ...Most people want the illusion

My response...
You are right I live in fairy tale land

Mr. Jones...

How many people have told you what I just said?

My response
No one.

Mr Jones, Exactly you need a chance to look at you. What you have discovered about you is that you don't want to discover you. You are so into the illusion that you don't want to discover your pair of shoes.

You know who that hurts?

My reply, "Moi."

Mr. Jones, Yes, because you run away from yourself and that is the only one that you don't want to learn. You.

You are looking for an answer outside of yourself. When you need to take the time to give yourself a chance, you need to be true to yourself and then people will be true to you.

*"If you take the artist away it is like taking the water out of your life. Artist are more valuable than anything"*

Looking inside yourself is a great start, before you expect others to do what you in fact are unwilling to do.

My response, It has been so hard for me to look at myself, trust myself, and the fact that I failed to put complete trust in God this is why I have not truly succeeded to the place where I should be.

Mr. Jones Don't look at things as a form of success or failure, because the real answer comes from being true to yourself and allowing yourself to discover the real you.

My response, *"That is truly amazing indeed."* As we finish up this interview Mr. Jones concerning the story of your siblings as you were lining up to get a whooping it is obvious that you encountered the cost at an early age and became willing to pay it for yourself.

Mr. Jones, I started drawing when I was little I stop getting whooping for a whole week. I just knew that I did not want to get one.

It took a lot of pain away from what would have been to me that is a huge blessing. Now add up all these years of how much pain it could have been, but it help rescue me. It kept me on track.

### Q. WHAT WAS THE QUESTION THAT YOUR MOTHER ASKED YOU AND YOUR SIBLINGS?

A. The question was, What do you want to be when you grow up? You had to know what you were talking about, you have to remember she had a long white switch in her hand waiting to come down on you.

1. Believe

2. Love

3. Care about what they did

4. Visualize your finish product of how good it is going to be

5. Knowing brought on a confidence. A flow-they knew

6. Nature flows at its own pace.

7. Let it be. Substance is what makes stuff and people fall in love with it.

8. If you stand you will eventually gain.

I believe that the spirit of my father spoke through this man to moi at my time of need. I was desiring to hear my fathers voice, but instead I met a man with his name.

# confession 40

## TROPHY WIFE

"Every man of a certain status wants a #trophywife because he knows that she looks the part and she is smart enough to play the game."

Despite what we all think ladies if it is fairy tale you want, it is fairy tale you must give. Every man who is of a certain caliber wants a "trophy wife" sort of speak, whether it is his girlfriend, lady, woman, or wife.

We all know what she is, however most of us do not know how she acts. She can be an asset or a liability to a man of greatness.

#1 If she is an asset she comes with wisdom, knowledge, virtue, and understanding.

#2 If she is a liability everything on the outside of her is great & her insides are no good. She has a bad attitude, no understanding, & she lacks all wisdom.

Now a man judges #1 & #2 to be the same when he see's both of them. They both stand a chance right off the bat with this man type personality. He has places to go, people to meet, awards to receive, & limo's to ride to the airport in. When he walks in that 5 star hotel he wants her on his side. When he attends the biggest dinner meeting of the year & prepares to celebrate with his new clients later he wants his "trophy wife" there. When he is receiving a high achievement, performance, nominee award, or Grammy award he wants you there to show off how great his life is in its entirety. This man is all about "living a lifestyle" with his trophy wife. This is how he will be with you.

The kicker ladies once he realizes that you are a #2 no matter how great you look, you must go. You cannot stay in the life of this personality long, because this man does not want to risk his success to the hands of a woman that will damage what he has built. You will damage his career. You are not an asset.

> "A man wants sex. A King wants respect + sex."

Lady #1 you are here to stay. The only issue with you is that you are so wonderful that he will soon not trust you. Your struggle will be to constantly work to earn the trust of this man. You are so beautiful, so smart, business minded, & you will make an awesome mother figure–there is no way this guy wants to release you from your life therefore the best next thing for him to do is to man up. He wants to marry you. These type of women are blessed with a blessing and a curse. You mean well, but the world says that, "You are too good to be true." Your battle will become a long journey. You will experience the most hardship in relationships than the average woman, however know that when this much greatness exist that so does your Boaz.

Boaz is the one man that sees your beauty outside and inside, yet he understands that your value is far above rubies. He will respect you, while other men want you for sex. Boaz wants you lying at his feet with respect. A man wants sex. A King wants respect + sex.

We get so caught up in the outside that we forget what is of value to a man of royalty. A man of royalty will never be satisfied with worldly pleasures. Below are a list of worldly pleasures:

1. If you are beautiful outside & you have nothing of substance going for you. Worldly.

2. We like to wear make-up, but they want to see your natural face. {I know this is a kicker. I love make-up, however this is the truth about this man of royalty. He see's you as a beauty with it and without it.

3. He does not like woman with boob jobs. Sorry not plastic surgery with this "man of royalty". He is more than happy with nature & all that is natural. You better pray for increase.

4. He can afford a $50 million dollar home or even higher, however the only reason that this "man of

royalty" would consider buying this home is for you "Queen."

He is content with the little things.

5. He does not want to see you twerking on your timeline, nor does he wants the world to see you as he does. You must be covered.

6. He desires his Queen to be better than him, to teach him, to speak words of truth unto his spirit, and to remind him of his true self.

Being a trophy is all well and good, but at some point desire to spend your life with someone of substance.

# confession 41
## ENTER INTO THE SOUL OF THE DIVINE

"Enter into the soul of the I am that I am. Be confident about the person that God created you to be."

Love is a gift that is meant to be embraced, not forced. When you force anything, it becomes and is completely unnatural and unlawful. The phrase, "I am, that I am," is such a powerful, yet amazing phrase. It reveals much intelligence and confidence. It is easily to be entreated, not easy in the sense that anyone can have it, but easy as in breathe taking, delightful, and filled with true intimacy.

The person that is connected to the soul of God, even as you are will understand certain details of the kingdom.

### FEMALE: QUEEN

She sets the environment for her King. (Burn candles, aroma in the air, clean)

She prepares a table for her King. [ She can cook and she is willing to feed her King when he is hungry.

She trust that her King will take care of her.

She speaks wisdom and truth.

She teaches her children real love.

### MALE: KING

He opens the Queens door, to remind that he always goes before her to prepare a place.

He is protective over his Queen He guards her life, as it is his own.

He loves to share ½ of all he has with his Queen.

He gives his Queen confidence that he will do as he says. He is a man of action and a man of his word.

How do you enter into the soul of the divine?

The question is not posed for those who are already walking in the knowing of the answers, it is for those who have not found it yet. If you want to improve your love life naturally you will be required to do things differently. If you don't allow things to flow naturally it will only create problems such as:

1. Cause arguments
2. Creates tension in the home
3. Brings more separation
4. Increases the likelihood of failure in the relationship
5. Creates trust issues

Who wants any of those problems? None of us, right? We all have been keen to creating and starting these horrible situations for no apparent reason, besides the one that exist in our mind alone.

Where is your Queen (in you)?

Where is your King (in you)?

It is time to put love into practice. We all desire to experience love, however are we willing to do what it takes for us to operate in love? We feel the need to protect ourselves verses our partner. When you feel the need to defend yourself all the time, there is definitely an issue that exist in you. What issues could possibly exist in you when you are on the defense all the time?

*Reason #1*

Insecure, you fear being left by your partner. This comes from something or someone in your childhood that left you or a relationship that did not work out. These left broken feelings in you about relationships.

*Reason #2*

You are doing something wrong that you know that you should not be doing. You are on the defense, because you fear your own karma.

*Reason #3*

You don't know how to love, so you don't love your partner. This can be dangerous, because those who don't take the time to figure this out within their self often miss out on someone great loving them.

There could be many reason why your partner or yourself is on the defense including the loss of a friend, or sibling, or a parent. You want to make sure that if any of these are the issue that you stay in constant prayer for your partner. God is able to remove pain, bitterness, and anger, but you will have to operate in wisdom in order for this to happen.

# confession 42

## WOMEN DESIRE TO BE GUIDED

"A real woman ra'spects her man's leadership, she craves it."

Oh what a feeling it is when the man you love can touch you from within and he has never even touched your flesh. He has no addictions. He speaks truth to your spirit and has an exclusive connection to your soul that no one else in this world has.

There is a man that has your best interest at heart and in mind with no evil intentions to you or towards you. His thoughts are that of God.

There are men who never get this far, because they have not taken the time to connect to the soul of God. You have to become spiritually in-tune to the spirit to know what is taking place between the two of you.

When a man or a woman is connected to the soul of God they will know not only when you are happy, sad, upset, they will know when to fill you back up.

A man walking in this type of anointing will increase your energy level, he won't compete with you, and he has no need of spoil. In fact he has a managerial spirit to ensure that what God gives you will remain yours plus more.

{Where does guidance come from?}

In order for you to be led, there must already be an existing connection between God, you, and your partner. Once that connection is there, you will experience growth, love, and romance beyond your wildest imagination.

## MOVIES THAT I MUST CONFESS I LOVE

*'Dirty Dancing'* is one of my favorite movies, because it teaches you so much if you pay attention. One of the biggest issues that the movie deals with is fear. As humans we hate to admit that fear could house itself in our temple. The female (main character) in the movie had fear that caused her to become stiff, rigid, and it kept her from being free with her partner. Fear is a factor in many of today's relationships. The fact that it is makes moi pose this question, *"What if fear was not a factor at all?" Would you become one with your partner?*

The movie goes on and you begin to see their issues, different backgrounds, a man who use to be your typical ladies man, received a disapproval from her family. He had different goals, and different friends. In fact the only common ground they had was the fact that they understood one another through their desire to love, their hearts were connected, and there was passion in between the two of them.

These are usually barriers that fear causes us to avoid. The pressure of all these issues can make or break a relationship. You must exercise a huge amount of tolerance and strength to overcome these barriers.

# LAW OF LOVE

*"Only a strong love can ultimately overcome barriers."*

Fear is not real. We have a hard time believing this, yet it is true. Fear is only something that we perceive in our minds to be true. If we held on to fear, it would keep us from loving, and becoming one with our partner and expanding in our love.

Often times fear is placed there by the two of you when neither one of you know how to love. This is like living in a nightmare. You want to keep an open spirit, because that will open you up to a mutual open partnership. Your goal is for the two of you to overcome your fears together. The worse thing that you can do is to make a decision to live the same day everyday for the rest of your life. *"Never live the same day twice"-Monster* in Law

When I heard that statement in this movie, I received it immediately. You should not be afraid to do something different alone or with your partner. Life is about living it. Whether your live it alone or with a partner just live, stop worrying about everything that could go wrong. Focus on being what you desire and attract it in your life.

> **"Never live the same day twice"**
> –Monster in Law

Life is not always planned, in fact the best moments that I have ever experience were unplanned. Life has given you an opportunity to live it up everyday. It can take a lifetime to meet your love partner, so in the mean time spend the time loving the life that you are living.

I went through a lonely period in my life, this time was about moi learning to love myself. I hated this time.-Confession of a love goddess.

Although this time was somewhat difficult I learned a lot about moi. There is nothing wrong with taking things slow to learn who you are. There is nothing worse than bringing your possible life partner down with your own confusion. Knowing who you are, what you want, before you make any request known unto a partner.

Love is experienced best when you are ready for it. The problem is that we think we are ready too soon without even hearing from the spirit of God. This was my problem. I desired love, family, but I didn't know who God wanted for moi.

We also make the mistake of believing that our relationship will be perfect. All these are thoughts that come from your fears.

In the movie "Monster in Law" Jennifer Lopez who played the main character, met her soon to be mother in law who was pretending to like her for the sake of her son. Ladies we are all too familiar with this, but you know deep down inside she has been out to destroy your relationship since Day 1.

The mother tried everything including embarrass her future daughter in law, hurt her feelings, work to break her down, make her feel like she was nothing, and the worse thing about it was that she was a control freak. She was a soon to be bride that was living a nightmare!

A mother like this is obsessed with her son, which is by far the worse feeling in the world. If you say something to the Mom she will deny it, and the son will think you are being paranoid. It is hard when you experience this because to the son, momma dearest can do no wrong. This is a situation where a son has not learned to step out on faith into his manhood.

This is a test of true love when your relationship can overcome these harsh barriers. We were taught a man who loves his momma will surely love you, but what about a momma who seems to be in love with her son? Spooky! Out of order! Way too much!

## LAW OF LOVE

"Be strong and secure enough in your love that you see the enemy when he presents himself in anyone."

The person that is connected to the soul of God, even as you are will also understand certain details of the kingdom.

# confession 43

## LOVE IS GOING TO WIN
## #lovewins

*"Everyone is praying for that special someone that they can vow to love forever and mean it."*

Is it all just make believe when it comes to love?

Does for better or worse just hold true to marriage or is it a vow to love? At some point we fathom that our life is connected to the awesome vow to loving someone other than yourself. As hard as that may seem for us to do so it is possible for us to reach outside of our own selfishness and love someone other than ourselves.

When you make a vow to be with someone that you know that you love and you know that you would do nothing to intentionally harm this person. We are all big boys and big girls we know that some relationships we didn't care how we made the other person feel, but anytime you meet someone and you care enough to consider them and become cautious of their heart. This will become the time that you begin to take heed to vowing to loving them forever.

Throw the spirit of selfishness out of the window, you will not succeed this way. The only way to succeed is to focus on building the money and the empire. If something comes to distract you, then go back to the drawing board and keep building.

Trust yourself, trust in the love that exist, and don't doubt it for one moment. You have this on lock but you must be loyal to the commitment that you have made to one another, and most importantly you must be loyal to the commitment that you have made with yourself.

One of the most influential person in my life walked away when I was a little girl and today as an adult woman he remains one of the most influential person in my life. I grew up feeling alone by his absence. I felt like I needed him to be apart of my life, like him being there would have helped my life make sense in some type of way. I was angry with a man that I had never really known. A man that I felt like was supposed to protect moi from this pain called life.

The pain grew in my heart into un-forgiveness. How could I ever forgive someone who never thought about moi another day in his life? There were so many thoughts going through my head, the older that I got the more those thoughts just grew stronger within mind.

So one day I finally build up the nerve to find him, to contact him. The phone rings, he answer, "Hello."

I am in silence as he repeats, "Hello."

"Hi, this is your daughter."

"He replies, who?"

"Your daughter."

This is the moment when my heart crushes, because as he proceeds to speak I realize that he is acting to have no memory of moi. I knew that it could only be an act, because there is no parent in his world that can forget their child even if they chose to block

them out of their life, mind, and heart. It still did not change the fact that he was hurting moi with such little words.

He proceeded to speak...."Is this your number?"

I responded, "Yes."

He says, "I am going to lock it in and save it."

This was the end of the conversing that we exchange between one another. I felt embarrassed, more pain, and even more hurt that a man who is a part of you could act as if you were nothing in his life.

It took moi years to understand and embrace the fact that I loved a man that I hardly knew but loved with a huge part of moi. I love my Dad even though he was not around. I didn't just love him for him, I love him for moi. This was all that I had of him and I had to be the one that allowed my thoughts of him to be love instead of pain. I could not allow any longer for this world to take from moi my love for my own dad regardless of what decisions that he made with his life. His choices had no barrier on moi choosing to make the right ones.

I knew first hand that being a parent is hard especially when you are only learning to be a man yourself. My dad was learning and he just never slowed down to think about the effects that his decisions had on moi or anyone else. He just kept going.

Weeks prior to moi completing this book...

I was attending a meeting with a business partner of mine about trades and investments and little did I know that the guy that was doing the presentation was from Indiana had a brother that he was in town visiting. When his brother walked into the room of the meeting I recognized him. I had meet him a couple years ago with Mr. Robert Jones. At that time he was discussing the power of real love. I recorded him speaking. I remembered clearly because he spoke with such intelligence and wisdom. He was an older man that went by the name of Andrew. I knew that it was nothing but the mere spirit of God that was bringing his spirit, his presence around for moi to gain a greater understanding of love.

Being the inquisitive woman that I am, I knew that I would soon begin to probe by asking more questions. I could not allow this divine moment to pass in my life without gaining more knowledge, wisdom, and understanding. The question was right there and somehow I had the hardest time of reaching a place or a level of release. I knew what I wanted to say, however saying it would not pour out. There I was and there the question that came, *"How do men love?"* I wanted to know was it something different about the way that they love and the way that woman love. Mr. Andrew got quiet momentarily, then he proceeded to speak.

*"Have you ever heard someone say that a piece of a man is better than no man?"*

I responded, *"Yes I have."*

Well, when God created Adam he created a piece of a man, when he created Eve she was taken from man's rib. She is a piece of a man. You are part man. You came from man. All men are a piece of a man until they discover the woman that is their rib. She is the one in whom shall make him whole. She is the other part of him. That is important. He said that he was never a whole man until he met his wife. I wanted to ask him how he felt as a man since he wife had just passed away, however I didn't want to be inconsiderate.

He continued to speak, *"You see a woman has no choice, man choses. She is XX, he is XY. The man chooses the woman."* A man with an extra 'Y' which is the XXY. He is a super male. He is tall in height and very masculine. This was a very interesting point that he brought up.

Understanding is a huge part of life. I was discovering a different sense of myself, my sensitivity, and my reasoning for desiring more understanding. Before long the conversation was about to increase. I am not sure that I was even prepared for what the spirit was releasing within moi at all. Mr. Andrews brother began to speak and what hit home so hard was when he began to speak about Fathers. He asked if my father was in my life growing up. I told him that he was not in my life and that has had a major affect on moi and I was feeling even more sensitive about the issue the more I came close to completing this book.

No matter how bad I thought I wanted to move on from the thoughts, my heart ached from my father not being around were still very much there. I was still holding on to him for as long as I could for the life of moi. I wanted to talk to him, I wanted to hear him, and I wanted to know him. If I could feel this way about a man that I have never really spent much time with, he had to be a huge part of moi. The fact that I knew that I loved this man, my father, my dad. It let moi know that there was someone in this world that I could love with no conditions. My love for him was unconditional.

For a man that I had never known had shown moi how to love no matter what he could do my love would remain the same. This man, this strange man spiritually was still able to show moi how to love without having any control over, in it. My dad taught moi that I could love someone, that I could love myself, and that I could love him, and others without them being presence, without them doing or being what I wanted them to be for moi.

God foresaw moi as being a controlling woman, this was Gods way of breaking moi. He blessed moi with a father that would freely teach moi that my love was not for moi it was for him, for others, for my family, and for my friends. My love was in my life for God to show others that love could exist when others would do their worse, be their worse, and without them even knowing that they were even doing.

More than anything I wanted to tell my father that I loved him and that I have always loved him, and that my love for him would remain for him for a lifetime. I wanted to tell him that him not being there was ok and that whatever mistakes he made had no reflection or barrier on the love I wanted to share with him.

This was preparation for what God would birth through my life next, my bio. I am not sure the date of release, but I do know the title. More than a last man's name I want to tell the world, "I am Miss Jones, my fathers daughter." I made several mistakes, but so have we all. Those mistakes don't determine any of our endings. We have no control over our endings and we have no control over our love.

All these years, all this time. I remembered this memory that my grandmother shared with moi: A promise ring that would symbolize my fathers' promise to always love moi forever. He committed to loving moi, but not the way that I thought that love was. He committed to loving moi without any control of how my life would turn out. He loved moi enough to let moi go and to let love win. Love won. Love made a decision a long time ago to not let moi go. I knew that if love had let moi go that I would not still feel the love so strongly. What is in a man's heart will also be in a man's mind. It has been on my mind, because my love for him will forever remain in my heart.

As a woman I learned to understand that sometimes the ones who just keep going are the ones who are facing the most adversity and the most pain. I found myself plenty of times in my own life in the mode to just keep going. It became my motto, my way of surviving, my way of holding on, my way of coping, and my way of living. I did not like to deal with things myself, especially if the things that I needed to deal with required moi

# Defeat does not exist in the will or the power of love.

facing the pain that I felt. This is why I no longer blamed my dad, his pain belonged to him not to moi.

This is when I chose to embrace the power of letting go and allowing love to win. You can have hope in any situation as long as you hold on to the fact that love is going to ultimately win. Defeat does not exist in the will or the power of love.

Many times those who see the most in you, are the ones who understand loving unconditionally.

a poem to my father
"Daddy I love you"

to all fathers never question how valuable you are to your little girl for when she gets older she will never forget the value that you are to her. you are a very important piece to the puzzle called love and the more she knows of your love for her the easier it is to accept love for her real king. don't let her spend her life wondering and trying to find out why you were not there to protect her from the not knowing. don't let her find out the hard way.

   lost in the body of a woman
   she's wondering what man wants her
   some man put he wrong image in her head
   infested with suggestions as the life that was supposed to love her put her away instead
   an idea of god is an in-equality ideology of a philosophy of a life chosen to just be a joke

you lost her at the moment when you told her life would possibly be broken with long suffering she thought your promise was heaven with no tears

now she is angry, destruction in her pathways

lessons of evil is what you have taught her

there she stands the age of youth between you and her

ever since she has been broken and mad at the little girl because you took her identity

now she stands a woman trapped with this little girl within, caught up with the mis-trust

every time this little girl pops up so does the idea of mis-trust

angry because her little girl is now a woman

a hurting reflection of her own rejection

bruised by the heel wondering why has it took so long for the little girl that was divided to be chosen to speak

nobody has spoken to moi

so how she speaks peace for wholeness to the nation to empower moi with the life of this kingdom there is a reason why daddy left you with this priceless life

and now that your little girl is in love

she understands that he felt so that your life would be better off without the brokenness

as he puts pieces of himself here and there of his brokenness so he breaks hearts because one injury made his whole world fall apart

this whole time i have been praying for mommy and moi

but daddy i never saw the fact that you were broken since the beginning

told that it was over, feeling like you would not amount to nothing

instead of mounting up as an eagle

feeling as though the precious mother and child would be better off

god if you could do one thing, please free this king

i love you daddy since the day that you left

who hurt you mommy?

they hurt moi too

when you see moi, you see the broken pieces of your heart

this is my reality

i am the thoughts of the voice that you refused to speak

yes i am the abuse that you kept hidden

i am the broken vessel that refuses to stop fighting

i am the prophetical anointing that is upon your life

nations are within moi

mommy i love you

as i stand there between the two of you, your brokenness

bye daddy!

my first negative image of a man in my head {the negative thoughts that i have been fighting}

mommy you thought it was just you, however i was broken too

i stood daughter between one nation as they became separated
i have lived an entire life in fear of losing a man
and what i fear manifested in my hand

ever since then daddy your little girl has been wondering if he walks out would her king return
at this moment she faces her reality

i am worthy of love, life, and justice
i am goddess
whole with the king in moi
so daddy if i never see you again
please know that the king lives in moi.

{Though I never had the opportunity I have been able to live my life in now knowing that the first king has never left moi -God. I fear not, therefore I am able as a woman to stand in the power of the love that is within moi.}

# Afterword

After all of my 43 Confessions, I felt like there was something still missing in my life. My main objective was striving for higher levels of success and when I felt that was not the way that I desired I felt like I wanted love badly this is when I realized that I was a not only #spoiled but a #loveaddict waiting for it to be quenched when no one had the power to quench it. I was addicted to the idea of love and the only thing and way that I could fulfill it was to not to date but to write. I fell more in love with moi from within. I did not want anymore disappointments in my personal life. I did not want to even chance it. So many of us think that the only addictions that exist is bad drug habits, sex, alcoholism, abuse but there are some individuals who are addicted to having that right special someone who may not be perfect but that are perfect for them.

That special someone is moi. I have given of myself to others for them to unappreciated moi. God gave moi the gift of love to love moi and to free myself. Until you value the love that God has given you forget anyone else valuing it. Life, love, and living is all about you. This book was just a personal journey for moi. I chose to share that journey with my readers. Through writing this book I gave myself courage to free myself to the land of the unknown.

Maybe all of us are fighting to be accepted of something but for moi the greatest acceptance that I could have ever made was accepting myself for who I am not what I did not have, and not for the things I missed out on. I accept the fact that my life is how it was intended to be and I am the only one who can control how great it is and how much greater it can be. Love is also a choice, well living in it is an entirely different subject. Be happy with your own greatness and one day you will meet an individual filled with the same greatness and together you can release more happiness into the lives of one another along with everyone who encounters the awesome power of love itself.

For if nothing else I truly understand this.

## "For without love & trust I am nothing & I have nothing."

It is to be remembered that in all your pain there is glory. There was something fighting moi my entire life to give up on love and how special it would be to moi. It was a very painful journey, many nights I felt as though I did not have the will to fight for it any longer, yet the will in moi remained to be 10 times stronger than what was going on around moi. I hated the pain. I could not understand its purpose, but now today I stand in love with the ability to share something so profound, so amazing that I just thank and praise God for giving moi the strength to keep going. You never know the depths of what is in front of you that is why it is so important for you to keep going. The spirit of God never gave up on moi fighting for the love within myself. For this I will forever be grateful that God's spirit thought enough of moi for moi to receive the sweetest gift #love.

I think that what makes life so interesting is the not knowing part. We don't even know if anyone is in our life for a lifetime. The truth is that maybe we are all just passing through, maybe our biggest challenge in life is facing that some individuals are temporarily passing through our life.

I believe that one day we will meet our soul mate if this is what we desire. I believe that our soul mate is someone that two individuals both can mutually agree that they want to be a part of one another's life for as long as possible. There is no biological time frame or clock that says when you know who this person is, however when the time is right the both of you will know.

More than anything or anyone I began to see that I was fighting for my own freedom with no judgments, no care, no wonder, and no worry. You must know that no one can truly set you free only the love that you have inside of you can do that. Although I wanted for all those who were in my life or are in my life to be apart of my success, I had to learn to not be so attached that I desired love more than I was content with love. Love yourself first!

I really do #Luv you.

Author's Bio

Born in 1979, in Ouachita Parish, Louisiana, raised in a small home in the country side of Epps, Louisiana with grandparents-Sarah & Al Humes. Where she saw two separate individuals love one another as one. This gave her a foundation to build upon until life challenged her to understand what that truly meant in the terms of 'true love.' This is how Humes became a hopeless romantic at heart. As painful as her journey in love has been she has never given up on the fact the truth about love and relationships exist in each of us.

Today she combines her love for family, life, beauty, fashion, lifestyle traveling, and writing to living her dreams to the fullest. Life Coach, Designer, Brand Consultant and Author of Success is What You Make it, Happy Endings Vol I., & The PR Plan, Founder of Luxury PR Boutique-RBR PR & Advertising Agency, Humes Luxury *Intl.* along with many other of her boss endeavors. Currently she is residing in the US.

monisoihumes.co

# YES FOLLOW MOI

It remains a goal of mine to connect with my readers. I have shared important parts of my life, not because I feel like there is anything new to be taught but that each one of us has a different message to deliver. My goal is to write as often as I can to share with you the ups and downs of my life to inspire you to have your own hope to keep going regardless of what your situation looks like. The spirit of God is the only thing that kept moi going and still keeps moi going when the rest of the world tried to show moi otherwise. I truly hope that the "43 CONFESSIONS OF A LOVE GODDESS" imparted something in your spirit. I hoped that it also made you laugh.

*MonisoiHumes.co*

# KEEPING UP WITH MONI'SOI HUMES

Available on Amazon, Barnes & Noble Dot com, Books A Million, Indie Bound Books

**Happy Endings: Vol I. Love Does Win**

ISBN-13: 978-0692629970

ISBN-10: 0692629971

**The PR Plan {The ultimate guide to owning your own brand}**

ISBN-13: 978-0692403754

ISBN-10: 0692403752

Business & Economics / Public Relations

**Success is What You Make It**

ISBN-13: 978-1492305781

ISBN-10: 1492305782

Self-Help / Personal Growth / Success

# Important Contacts

National Domestic Hotline
1(800-799-7233)

National Coalition Against Domestic Violence, NCADV
Website: ncadv.org

Washington Office (Public Policy)
2000 M Street NW, Suite 480
(202) 467-8714
publicpolicy@ncadv.org

Denver Main Office
1 Broadway, Suite B210
Dener, Co 80203
(303) 839-1852

American Foundation of Suicide Prevention
Walk Out of Darkness
Website: afsp.org

National Office
Toll Free: 1 (888) 333-AFSP (2377)
T (212) 363-3500

General inquiries:
info@afsp.org

Mailing address:
120 Wall Street
29th Floor
New York, NY 10005

National Suicide Prevention Hotline
1 (800) 274-TALK (8255)

# References

The Five Love Languages/Author/Gary Chapman/Quality Time /page 60

http://www.ncadv.org/learn/statistics

Canfield, Jack/ http://jackcanfield.com/transformation/

Brennan, Bridget/Forbes Contributor/Article/http://www.forbes.com/sites/bridgetbrennan/2015/01/21/top-10-things-everyone-should-know-about-women-consumers/#6753d92a2897 / Accessed-02-28-2016

http://sites.psu.edu/jyh5445/2013/12/08/brainwashed-by-barbie-what-a-doll
http://www.mamamia.com.au/i-found-this-today-on-my-daughters-floor-my-daughter-is-seven/

www.mint.com

If you are interested in receiving more advice or in booking the author for speaking engagement of book signing, please submit your request at booking@monisoihumes.co

If you are in a dangerous situation please 911 immediately; for legal advice please contact a Lawyer.

SOCIAL MEDIA **FACEBOOK** /IAmMonisoiHumes **TWEET MOI** @mhumes **IG** @monisoihumes **LINKED IN** in/monisoihumes **YOU TUBE** /user/soilifestyle **ITUNES** Soi Lifestyle by MONI'SOI HUMES.

www.ingramcontent.com/pod-product-compliance
Lightning Source LLC
Chambersburg PA
CBHW060351190426
43201CB00044B/2002